THE

FIFTH GOSPEL

A Verse-by-Verse
New Age Commentary
on the
Gospel of Thomas

ROBERT WINTERHALTER

1817

HARPER & ROW, PUBLISHERS, SAN FRANCISCO
Cambridge, Hagerstown, New York, Philadelphia, Washington
London, Mexico City, São Paulo, Singapore, Sydney

FIRST EDITION

Library of Congress Cataloging-in-Publication Data

Winterhalter, Robert, 1936–
  The Fifth Gospel.

  1. Gospel of Thomas—Criticism, interpretation, etc.
I. Gospel of Thomas.   II. Title.
BS2860.T52W54   1988   229'.8   87-45728
ISBN: 0-06-250972-1 (pbk.)

88 89 90 91 92 HC 10 9 8 7 6 5 4 3 2 1

TO

DR. JOSEPH BAUER

Mentor, professor, friend, and brother in Christ

Contents

Introduction

The discovery of the Nag Hammadi library in Egypt (1945) must be ranked as one of the major archaeological finds of the twentieth century. This collection contains valuable data regarding Christian origins and the early development of the church. It also adds greatly to our knowledge of the "gnostic" movements of the second and third centuries A.D. The word *gnostic* is derived from the Greek term *gnōsis*, which means "direct or immediate knowledge." There was never a single gnostic movement as such; the groups so designated had the greatest diversity of teachings. They all sought in some way, however, to extend their awareness to include extraphysical planes of reality.

The works in the Nag Hammadi collection, found buried near the Egyptian town of Nag Hammadi, apparently belonged to an early Christian monastery whose ruins have been found in the area. The site was once occupied by followers of Pachomius, the founder of Egyptian monasticism. It is likely that the monks, accused of heresy, buried the library to save it from destruction by the authorities.

The library in question is so diverse that it defies any attempt to summarize its contents, short of listing all of its fifty-two texts. A "common thread," however, runs through all of them. As James M. Robinson, the director of the Coptic Gnostic Library Project, has written,

The focus that brought the collection together is an estrangement from the mass of humanity, an affinity to an ideal order that completely transcends life as we know it, and a life-style radically other than common practice. This life-style involved giving up all the goods that people usually desire and longing for an ultimate liberation. It is not an aggressive revolution that is intended, but rather a withdrawal from involvement in the contamination that destroys clarity of vision.[1]

The subject of my book is one member of this library, the Gospel of Thomas. As Robinson also affirms,

This collection [the Gospel of Thomas] of some 114 sayings attributed to Jesus is certainly the most important part of the library for understanding the historical Jesus and the beginnings of Christianity. It alone would make the Nag Hammadi library a very important discovery, probably doing more as a single text to advance our understanding of the historical Jesus and of the transmissions of his teachings than all the Dead Sea Scrolls put together.[2]

Thomas begins with the statement "These are the secret sayings which the living Jesus spoke and which Didymos Judas Thomas wrote down."

The Gospel of Thomas, as we now have it, shows the hand of an Egyptian editor. Two facts are important to note. First, this editor translated the document from Greek into Coptic, the native language of Egypt in late antiquity. Second, the editor also changed some of the sayings to bring them into agreement with his own frame of reference. His edition is—as is also the case with the four canonical gospels—an interpretation. Therefore, to achieve the greatest possible clarity, we must seek to ascertain what frame of reference motivated this later editor. Although it is unwise to draw any hasty conclusions (as some scholars have done), it appears that his belief system more or less resembles that of the Nag Hammadi collection as a whole. Note especially that Thomas rests on an earlier Greek edition, which is closer to the original form of Jesus' statements. Fragments of this earlier edition still exist, a point to which we will return.

The question of the work's *original* author of the Greek version inevitably presents itself. According to tradition, the Apostle Thomas went to southern India at an early date. Certain Christians there trace the founding of their church communities to his missionary efforts. Thomas could, of course, have compiled a list of sayings before heading east, other material being added later. It is equally plausible, however, that the collection was made in Thomas's honor, and that the attribution of authorship is actually a form of dedication. This is the case with many New Testament books, which complicates the question of authorship.

In any case, the use of Thomas's name points to eastern Syria as the work's likely place of origin. Many of the Syrian Christians, in fact, thought of him as Jesus' twin brother. Also, in Saying 13, Jesus declares Thomas to be his spiritual equal:

Jesus said [to Thomas], "I am not your master. Because you have drunk, you have become intoxicated from the bubbling spring which I have measured out."

The bubbling spring represents the spiritual consciousness to which Jesus referred in a more frequently used metaphor: the kingdom of God. Viewed in a certain way, the Gospel of Thomas may seem to be a disorderly collection of sayings. If we view it, however, as expressing the inner kingdom of Christ Consciousness, most of its sayings reflect a common theme.

The Revised Standard Version of Luke 17:20–21 reads,

Being asked by the Pharisees when the kingdom of God was coming, he answered them, "The kingdom of God is not coming with signs to be observed; nor will they say, 'Lo, here it is!' or 'There!' for behold, the kingdom of God is in the midst of you."

By contrast, the King James Version closes this passage with the words "the kingdom of God is *within you*" (thus translating the Greek *entos humōn*). In this instance, the older translation, the King James, is correct. The structure of Luke 17:20–21 in Greek, as in English, plainly means that the kingdom of God cannot be limited to a given place. On the contrary, it is *entos*, meaning *"inside"*—a strengthened form of the preposition *en*, meaning "in." This does not mean in a physical sense, of course, but as a state of intuitive knowing that is received through one's consciousness. We either contact it there, or we do not have it at all. Luke's expression for "among" is *en mesō*, as in Luke 10:3: "Go your way; behold, I send you out as lambs in the midst of *[en mesō]* wolves."

The idiom *entos humōn* also meant "within your power" or "in your hands." The Divine Presence not only illumines the individual; it also empowers him or her to be and do all that God intends for him or her to be and to do. The kingdom, as Jesus understood it, is thus a combination of inner illumination and active dominion, the second being an expression of the first. Heaven is not a place but a state of consciousness.

The Greek text of the Gospel of Thomas agrees. Saying 3 states, in part, that the kingdom is within or inside of us (again, *entos humōn*). Then it equates the inner kingdom with knowing oneself; that is, *heautous gnōsesthe*, "you will know yourselves."

The Gospels of Matthew, Luke, and Thomas include many similar sayings.[3] At the same time, arguments made to show that the author of Thomas used the canonical gospels as a source are unconvincing. The Gospel of Thomas is thus of great significance as *a source for the teachings of Jesus that is independent of the Four Gospels.* "Believers" and "unbelievers" alike, however defined, must now reasonably conclude that Jesus existed as a historical person and presented at least some of the teachings attributed to him.

The resemblances among sayings in Matthew, Luke, and Thomas (and, to a lesser extent, between sayings in John and Thomas) must be accounted for in another way. Helmut Koester of Harvard University is correct when he concludes,

A comparison of the sayings in the *Gospel of Thomas* with their parallels in the synoptic gospels suggests that the sayings in the *Gospel of Thomas* either are present in a more primitive form or are developments of a more primitive form of such sayings. Indeed, the *Gospel of Thomas* resembles the synoptic sayings source, often called "Q" (from the German word *Quelle*, "source"), which was the common source of sayings used by Matthew and Luke. Hence the *Gospel of Thomas* and its sources are collections of sayings and parables which are closely related to the sources of the New Testament gospels.[4]

Nevertheless, many teachings in Thomas have no parallel in the Bible.

Most readers will find these "new" sayings to be of special interest. *They are significant because they support what is called the metaphysical view of Jesus' teachings.* Some sayings are spurious or greatly altered, but this is the work of the later Egyptian editor. And, while separating the true from the false is not easy, neither is it mere guesswork. The fragments of the Greek text of Thomas that still exist give us a reliable basis for comparing the Greek and the Coptic editions, and for more or less ascertaining the bias of the revised edition.

The fragmentary Greek papyri, three in number, were found near Oxyrhynchus, also in Egypt, in 1897 and 1903. Although they attracted some attention when they were first announced to the public, no one knew at the time that they were from the Gospel of Thomas. That they are indeed from Thomas becomes obvious by placing these Greek sayings side by side with the Coptic. The following chart shows the parallels between the Greek and Coptic manuscripts. Oxyrhynchus Papyri 654, 1, and 655 are abbreviated to OP.

GREEK	COPTIC
OP 654, lines 1–5	Preface, Saying 1
OP 654, lines 5–9	Saying 2
OP 654, lines 9–21	Saying 3
OP 654, lines 21–27	Saying 4
OP 654, lines 27–31	Saying 5
OP 654, lines 32–39	Saying 6
OP 654, lines 40–42	Saying 7
OP 1, lines 1–4	Saying 26
OP 1, lines 4–11	Saying 27
OP 1, lines 11–22	Saying 28
OP 1, line 23	Saying 29
OP 1, lines 24–31	Saying 30, 77
OP 1, lines 31–36	Saying 31
OP 1, lines 37–42	Saying 32
OP 1, lines 42–44	Saying 33
OP 655, lines 1–17	Saying 36
OP 655, lines 17–23	Saying 37
OP 655, lines 24–40	Saying 38
OP 655, lines 41–50	Saying 39

What remains of the Greek text is necessary to a full understanding of the Gospel of Thomas. In a few cases, variants of a given saying found in the Greek and Coptic texts may derive from separate sources. Almost always, however, the Greek form is earlier and more reliable.

Another relevant question is "What did the original compiler of Thomas use as a basis for selection?" Assuming that he or she had access to certain written material and oral traditions in memory, why did this compiler record sayings of a certain type and not others? It is helpful at this point to consider the early Christians of Eastern Syria, especially those in and near the city of Edessa. Their emphasis was substantially different from that in Syrian Antioch, where the Gospel of Matthew was compiled as a kind of church manual. For example, in Antioch the Christians came to view the Second Coming of Christ largely as an external event. The Christians in Edessa, however, focused on Jesus' teachings of inward illumination. If we consider the emphases of both documents, we find an obvious kinship of imagery and ideas between the Gospel of Thomas and the Odes of Solomon, a kinship that is not shared, to the same degree, by the Gospel of Matthew. Most of the work known as the Odes of Solomon is the product of an inspired soul in the first century A.D. These odes, and the sayings in Thomas, reflect a similar sense of Jesus' inner kingdom.[5]

Both the Gospel of Thomas and the Odes of Solomon have Jewish Christian affinities, although the later Egyptian editor somewhat blunted this influence in Thomas. Both documents share many expressions also used by the Essenes—reflecting similarities of style, theme, and imagery—although modified in a clearly Christian direction.

For instance, while the Odes of Solomon has its own distinct style, it shares with the Essene writings such motifs as eternal life, inner peace, intuitive knowledge, light/darkness, living water, love, truth, the Word, and world.

A comparison of the Odes of Solomon and Thomas yields an even more impressive list of common themes, including the themes and images of above/below, beginning/ending, bow (and arrow), drunkenness (as both a positive and a negative metaphor), ear(s), eye(s), fruit(s), hand(s), life/living, the Living One, light/darkness, know/knowledge, milk/suckling, persecution, rest/peace, secret, stripping/clothes, true/truth, water/river/thirst, world, and a yoke.

The New Testament includes four accounts of Jesus' teachings and ministry: Matthew, Mark, Luke, and John. Thomas adds a fifth significant source, hence its status as "the Fifth Gospel." Thomas has no narrative, and because of this lack of connecting events some have denied its status as a gospel. This objection, however, seems overly technical. The manuscript of the document ends with the words "The Gospel According to Thomas." Also, the sequence—indeed, sequences—in which events are presented in the canonical gospels are, to a large extent, a later reconstruction. Thomas, moreover, helps substantially to inform us of Jesus' teachings. Some authentic sayings, previously unknown, are found here. Its version of the parables is helpful in determining their original form, without the secondary settings in which the authors of Matthew, Mark, and Luke placed most of them.

Should the Gospel of Thomas, then, be included in the Bible? Even in its present Coptic form, it certainly qualifies as supplementary reading. Some caution is needed, of course, because of the Egyptian editor's changes. Apparently he did not fully share Jesus' vision of the Unity of Being, since the belief in a universe divided and in conflict was an important element in most Gnostic belief systems. With the progress of archaeology, however, who is to say that a more accurate text may not be found? If this possibility comes to pass, then certainly Thomas should be considered for admission into the New Testament.

Also, let us not be overly harsh on the Coptic editor. Although he and others of his school were awkward in the way they went about it, their goal of *attaining clarity of vision* is basically sound. It is of the essence of the purpose for which we have been created, as unfolding children of God.

Three technical points need to be made. First, the division of the Gospel of Thomas into exactly 114 sayings, though somewhat arbitrary, is adequate. As a matter of convenience, both for students and for the general reader, I have used the framework of 114 now accepted by the majority of scholars.

Second, I am using the division of the Odes of Solomon into verses developed by James H. Charlesworth. His critical text of the odes, together with his translation, are now definitive. Students who have copies of Rendel Harris's translation will note these differences.

Third, for the benefit of those who wish to explore the topic further, I have furnished appropriate sayings numbers from John Dominic Crossan's excellent guide, *Sayings Parallels: A Workbook for the Jesus Tradition* (Philadelphia: Fortress Press, 1986). This is a basic resource for individual and class work in comparing various versions of Jesus' sayings as found in the canonical gospels, the Gospel of Thomas, and other early extracanonical sources.

Two other books are highly recommended. One is Jack Finegan's *Hidden Records of the Life of Jesus* (Philadelphia: Pilgrim Press, 1969). It includes actual photographs of OP–654, OP–1, and OP–655, and shows the Greek text and English translation of all the sayings included in these fragments. The other is *Nag Hammadi, Gnosticism, and Early Christianity,* edited by Charles W. Hedrick and Robert Hodgson, Jr. (Peabody, MA: Hendrickson, 1986). Chapter 7, "On Bridging the Gulf from Q to the Gospel of Thomas (or Vice Versa)," by James M. Robinson, especially relates to the subject in hand.

The Fifth Gospel is written to begin an ongoing process, by a wider public, of the interpretation and use of the Gospel of Thomas. This amazing rediscovery, first appearing in 1945, helps point the way to the realization of the Inner Light, the Indwelling Christ, the kingdom of God that is within and yet among us. The author of Thomas would concur with this statement. May *The Fifth Gospel* be a stepping-stone to a deeper awareness of the Truth that sets us free.

The Gospel of Thomas

TEXT AND COMMENTARY

The Gospel of Thomas

PREFACE. *These are the secret sayings which the living Jesus spoke and which Didymos Judas Thomas wrote down.*

As I noted in the Introduction, no proof exists that the Apostle Thomas wrote down these sayings. Nevertheless, the use of Thomas's name reflects the high esteem that many Syrian Christians held for him.

The Gospel of Thomas contains essentially the same imagery and symbolism as the Odes of Solomon. The Odes were composed largely by a Jewish Christian of first-century Syria, although a few of them may date from early in the second century. The author of Thomas's basis of selection—from a much larger number of sayings available to him—was intuitive experience of the quality on which the Odes also are based.

The expression "the living Jesus" affirms his resurrection from the dead, as well as the eternal life of God that makes him a present fact. Luke 24:5–6 declares, "Why do you seek *the living* among the dead? He is not here, but has risen." John 14:19 assures us, "because I live, you will live also." Again, the glorified Christ of Revelation affirms, "Fear not, I am the first and the last, and *the living one;* I died, and behold I am alive for evermore" (Rev. 1:17–18).*

The Odes of Solomon repeat the theme of immortal life several times. For example,

> Indeed he who is joined to Him who is immortal,
> Truly shall be immortal.
> And he who delights in the Life
> Will become living.
>
> (Ode 3:8–9)

These words are given as from Jesus:

---

*All italicized words and phrases in Scripture are my emphasis unless otherwise noted.

And I gave my knowledge generously,
And my resurrection through my love.
And I sowed my fruits in hearts,
And transformed them through myself.
Then they received my blessing and lived,
And they were gathered to me and were saved;
Because they became my members,
And I was their Head.

(Ode 17:13–16)

Both the Gospel of Thomas and the Odes of Solomon have symbolic titles—an interesting common feature. To this day, King Solomon is best known for his wisdom. At the time, Solomon also was a miracle worker in the popular imagination. The Odes, however, do not emphasize that tradition. Rather, they give great emphasis to the themes of light, intuitive knowledge, and wisdom. This tradition goes back to various Old Testament passages. For example, 1 Kings 3:28 speaks thus of the wisdom of God in Solomon:

And all Israel heard of the judgment which the king had rendered; and they stood in awe of the king, because they perceived that the wisdom of God was in him, to render justice.

The Odes of Solomon declare that wisdom comes from God—in a deeper sense, it *is* God. For example, Ode 6:6 reads,

The Lord has multiplied His knowledge,
and He was zealous that those things should be known
which through His grace have been given to us.

The name Didymos Judas Thomas is a key to the central motif of the Gospel of Thomas. It is a way of saying, "A twin—praise God—a twin! In Greek, *didymos* means "a twin," and in Aramaic *thomas* has the same meaning. *Judah(-s)* means "Praise God." Many Syrian Christians thought of Thomas as the twin brother of Jesus! The mention of relationship, however, is symbolic. It means that *whoever* receives, and appropriates, the same inner awakening as Jesus becomes his practical equal. He is Jesus' twin, in that he becomes consciously of the same mind and substance in the Cosmic Christ.

Two other ancient documents speak of Thomas as the twin of Jesus. Both use the full formula, "Didymos Judas Thomas." These are the Acts of Thomas, a later product of the Syrian church; and the Book of Thomas the Contender, found in the Nag Hammadi collection. The latter work explains the symbolic meaning as follows:

Since it has been said that you are my twin and true companion, examine yourself that you may understand who you are, in what way you exist, and how you will come to be. Since you are called my brother, it is not fitting that you be ignorant of yourself. And I know that you have understood, because you had already understood that I am the knowledge of the truth. So while you accompany me, although you are uncomprehending, you have in fact already come to know, and you will be called "the one who knows himself." For he who has not known himself has known nothing, but he who has known himself has at the same time already achieved knowledge about the Depth of the All.[1]

There is, then, a basic shift of self-identity. At one stage, the soul looks "upward" to the Indwelling Christ as Savior, Guide, and Healer. After the shift within, the individual *is* the Christ, and looks "downward" on soul and body, pouring Its light and energy in and through all levels.

Both Thomas and the Odes of Solomon promote this shift. Thomas does so through its teachings alone. The Odes, in addition, do so by means of a liturgical device. A transition between the *me* and the "I AM," as it were, occurs in the Odes in eight places: 8:8, 10:4, 17:6, 28:9, 31:6, 36:3, 41:8, and 42:3. (This is in addition to Ode 22, which is written entirely from the "I AM" standpoint.) At these points, the Odists became identified with Jesus, and through him with the Indwelling Christ. They knew the Christ both as the Self, and as the fountain of individual life.

This shift is also the basis of true brotherhood. For in union with the Christ Mind, which is One, we find that our individual souls are joined. In this realization, we no longer view ourselves as separated minds, but as the One Mind functioning through various centers of consciousness. Here is the deeper sense of the Second Great Commandment: "You shall love your neighbor as yourself."

AFFIRMATIONS

—I have the Mind of Christ. I AM the Mind of Christ.

—I am heir to all the ideas in the infinite Mind of God.

—The radiant light of Christ surrounds me and illumines my path.

—I am alive with the Life of God. Through the Spirit of God in me, I am now responding to his healing Life and Love.

—I am a brother (sister) of Jesus the Christ, and of every man, woman, and child.

—Our minds are joined in the One Mind. I accept the peace of God.

---

1. *And he said, "Whoever finds the interpretation of these sayings will not experience death."(No. 242)**

---

*Throughout, the number that follows each saying in the Gospel of Thomas refers to the appropriate section in John Dominic Crossan's *Sayings Parallels: A Workbook for the Jesus Tradition,* which compares various versions of Jesus' sayings as found in the canonical gospels, the Gospel of Thomas, and other early extracanonical texts.

In John 8:51, Jesus declares, "Truly, truly, I say to you, if any one keeps my word, he will never see death." The statements in Thomas and in John, though different in form, are similar in meaning. As already noted, the interpretation or inner sense of the sayings in Thomas is based on the Indwelling Christ as our true Self. And in John, to "keep my word" *(logos)* means to abide continually in the Christ Self. To know our eternal spiritual Identity, and to unite with it, is to transform our present experience. We awaken to the fact that we are already in eternal life, and the fear of death disappears.

AFFIRMATIONS

—I abide consciously in the Logos, the Mind of Christ. I AM that Mind, and Its perfect expression in thought, body, and affairs.

—I am poised in peace and beauty. I rest in calm trust, and rely on the Indwelling Christ to bring good into my experience.

---

2. *Jesus said, "Let him who seeks continue seeking until he finds. When he finds, he will become troubled. When he becomes troubled, he will be astonished, and he will rule over the all." (No. 85)*

Two other versions of this saying exist. The Greek text of Thomas (OP 654, Lines 5–9) has some gaps. Clement of Alexandria preserves the third version, quoting from a work now lost, the Gospel According to the Hebrews. It is found in Clement's work, the Stromata. The most likely reconstruction of the saying's original form would be translated, "Let him who seeks continue to seek until he finds; when he finds, he will marvel; when he marvels, he will reign; and when he reigns, he will rest."

Thus in its Greek form, it is well attested as an authentic saying of Jesus. As in Matthew 7:7–11 and Luke 11:9–13, he who seeks finds. Jesus evidently gave it in Aramaic, for it follows a rhythmic structure that he often used. Its key terms made it easy to remember. They are (in English translation):

> seeks / finds
> finds / marvel
> marvels / reign
> reigns / rest

Matthew Black, an authority on the Aramaic background of Jesus' sayings, observes,

The sayings of Jesus are cast in the form of Semitic poetry, with such characteristic features as parallelism of lines and clauses, rhythmic structure, and possibly even rhyme. Parallelism and rhythm are more easily discernible than rhyme, the recognition of which is almost wholly conjectural. Parallelism of lines and clauses can be readily detected and studied even in translation.[1]

Saying 2, in both its Greek and Coptic forms, teaches that the search for Truth needs to be sincere and persistent. He who seeks will find, but only if he keeps at it. This follows Jeremiah the prophet, who declared, "You will seek me and find me; when you seek me with all your heart, I will be found by you, says the Lord" (Jer. 29:13–14).

The marvel or wonder of finding God—the paradox of the search—is in awakening to the fact that *God was here all the time.* Divine Love is available to meet every human need. All the resources of Divine Mind are ready to flow in and through us, as we are open to receive them. We find that we are an unlimited Idea.

"When he marvels, he will reign." When we release and apply what we have learned from within, we gain a new sense of power and dominion in our everyday lives. The health, harmony, and abundance of the Indwelling Christ are made manifest in and through us.

"When he reigns, he will rest." Jesus spoke fairly often of rest and inner peace. By *rest,* he meant conscious communion with the Divine Presence, and a calm trust that God will complete his good work in and through us. "You will find rest for your souls" (Matt. 11:29).

In the same spirit, the Odes of Solomon teach dominion through spiritual consciousness, and the peace and rest of God in us. For example, Ode 3:5–7 declares,

> I love the Beloved and I myself love Him,
> And where His *rest* is, there also am I.
> And I shall be no stranger,
> Because there is no jealousy with the Lord Most High and Merciful.
> I have been *united* to Him, because the lover has found the Beloved,
> *Because I love Him that is the Son, I shall become a son.*

AFFIRMATIONS

—I unite with Divine Reality as I become still, and let Spirit have its perfect way in and through me.

—I am an unlimited Idea of God. All the resources of Divine Mind flow in and through me, as I am open to receive them.

—Divine Love is active within me, to meet every need.

—I give thanks for the dominion of the Indwelling Christ in mind, body, and affairs.

—I rest in the consciousness of God's life, joy, and peace.

---

3. *Jesus said, "If those who lead you say to you, 'See, the kingdom is in the sky,' then the birds of the sky will precede you. If they say to you, 'It is in the sea,' then the fish will precede you. Rather, the kingdom is inside of you, and it is outside of* *you. When you come to know yourselves, then you will become known, and you will realize that it is you who are the sons of the living father. But if you will not know yourselves, you dwell in poverty and it is you who are that poverty." (Nos. 196; 272)*

In this statement, Jesus paraphrased Deuteronomy 30:11–14. There too, the sky and sea are mentioned. The word is in one's own mouth and heart. It reads,

For this commandment which I command you this day is not too hard for you, neither is it far off. It is not in heaven, that you should say, "Who will go up for us to heaven, and bring it to us, that we may hear it and do it?" Neither is it beyond the sea, that you should say, "Who will go over the sea for us, and bring it to us, that we may hear it and do it?" But the word is very near you; it is in your mouth and in your heart, so that you can do it.

The Word of God, in the true sense, is also the kingdom of God that is within. Jesus meant that the kingdom is not a place, but a state of consciousness. The Cosmic Christ is omnipresent, and can be contacted anywhere. Once found "inside of you," however, it is also found "outside of you." While the kingdom is indeed *within* an inspired soul, its results *show forth* in tangible ways.

Many have argued over the meaning of the phrase *entos humōn*, which appears both in Luke 17:21 and in the Greek text of Saying 3. As explained in the Introduction, it has been translated both "within you" and "in the midst of you." Although the first meaning is correct, this does not rule out the second, but includes it. An inner realization of the kingdom always has positive results. The mind is illumined, the body is healed, relationships are harmonized, and human needs are met. The Lord's Prayer itself states that the kingdom is to come, and the divine will is to be done, "as in heaven [within], so on earth [without]."

The Coptic editor changed the sense of the text by translating, "When you come to know yourselves, then you will become known." The fragmentary Greek text does not include the statement, "will become known," but rather "will discover this [that is, the kingdom]." The original saying affirms that knowing one's spiritual Identity is the equivalent of knowing God. There is no point to *becoming* known to God. For the Divine Intelligence, being unlimited in knowledge, already knows us fully, whether we are aware of this or not. Jesus' formula of identification assumes this truth. In another formula of identification, Paul declared,

For now we see in a mirror dimly, but then face to face. Now I know in part; then I shall understand fully, *even as I have been fully understood.* (1 Cor. 13:12)

To know ourselves as "sons of the living father" is true understanding. To fail to know our true selves, by contrast, is to "dwell in poverty." The Odes of Solomon also use poverty as a symbol of spiritual ignorance:

And ignorance appeared like dust,
And like the foam of the sea.
And vain people thought that it was great,
And they became like its type and were impoverished.
But the wise [literally, "those who knew"] understood
  and contemplated,
And were not polluted by their thoughts.

(Ode 18:11–13)

In summary, then, Saying 3 not only speaks of inner knowing, but also implies the importance of outer demonstration. We are not only to know the Truth, but to be energized by it. In ancient times, "within you" sometimes meant "in your power." Also, to be a "son of God" meant to be filled with power to do mighty works. So the two phrases reinforce each other. In the same spirit, John 1:12 (KJV) declares, "As many as received him, to them gave he power to become the sons of God, even to them that believe on his name."

AFFIRMATIONS

—The kingdom of God is within me.
—The consciousness of Truth works from center to circumference.
—It works in and through me to heal, to harmonize, and to adjust all that concerns me.
—It also works to heal and to bless all others with whom I come in contact.
—I see myself as God sees me, whole, strong, and well.
—I see myself as God sees me, wise, illumined, and making right decisions.
—I see myself as God sees me, capable, productive, and abundantly supplied.
—I am a son (daughter) of God within the Divine Sonship, the Cosmic Christ.

---

4. *Jesus said, "The man old in days will not hesitate to ask a small child seven days old about the place of life, and he will live. For many who are first will become last, and they will become one and the same." (Nos. 273, 170)*

Because a saying is absurd does not in itself mean that it is not authentic. Jesus sometimes used paradox and enigma to draw out deeper meanings from his hearers' psyches. Key images are the old man, the place of life, and the child of seven days.

In some contexts, an old man is an archetypal symbol of wisdom. A Greek term for "old," however—*palaios,* which Paul (and perhaps also Jesus) used—did not refer to a person's age as such, but had the sense of "worn-out, useless, decrepit." Unfortunately, the Greek fragment (OP 654, lines 21–27) is broken off and omits any terms for "old." However, Ephesians 4:22 tells the reader to reject the "old nature" [*ton palaion anthrōpon*], meaning the old negative self-image and belief system, which is false and tending toward disintegration. The soul can, however, find new birth on a higher level. This is the "child of seven days." The image expresses the archetype of the child—of new birth, growth, expansion. Seven is a symbol of perfection or completion.

The place of life is not a physical place, but a state of true understanding. This symbolic usage of *place* also occurs, for example, in the Gospel of John, the Gospel of Truth, and the Odes of Solomon. Also, a newborn infant is a suitable figure for two reasons. First, it has not yet learned to separate itself from its surroundings. Spiritual consciousness ("the place") is suprarational rather than prerational; yet it is analogous to infancy in the sense that it transcends the duality between subject and object. Also, the newborn does not use any words. This image implies that true understanding is *beyond* words, which do not convey it but merely point to the goal.

Saying 4 is in keeping with Jesus' imagery as in Luke 10:21 (see also Matthew 11:25), where he declares, "I thank thee, Father, Lord of heaven and earth, that thou hast hidden these things from the wise and understanding and revealed them to babes." He also tells us to become as little children, open and receptive. This does not mean simple-minded, but sincere and light-hearted in our acceptance of Divine ideas and guidance. Jesus emphasizes that such an attitude is necessary to spiritual rebirth:

Let the children come to me, do not hinder them; for to such belongs the kingdom of God. Truly, I say to you, whoever does not receive the kingdom of God like a child shall not enter it. (Mark 10:14–15)

The statement "For many who are first will become last, and they will become one and the same" is a variant of a saying of Jesus in Matthew 19:30, 20:16, Mark 10:31, and Luke 13:30. The Greek text of Saying 4 resembles the biblical form, declaring, "For many who are first will become last, and the last will be first, and . . . " At this point, the fragment breaks off. Since the Coptic ending, "and they will become one and the same," is not attested by any other source, it is doubtful.

The original saying, however, is certainly authentic. It is what may be called a "floater," and does not belong to the original context here. Also, its interpretation cannot be limited to a single meaning, for it is intentionally open-ended. It does refer, in a general way, to the reversal of human values and conditions that will occur when spiritual consciousness governs life on earth.

—I am open and receptive to the Truth, and I receive it joyously.

— I let go of worn–out, useless beliefs and attitudes. I am made new by the healing, inspiring action of the Christ within.

—I am renewed by the Christ Mind, created after the likeness of God in true right-mindedness and wholeness.

---

5. *Jesus said, "Recognize what is in your sight, and that which is hidden from you will become plain to you. For there is nothing hidden which will not become manifest." (Nos. 274; 115; 275)*

This is an authentic saying of Jesus. He is telling us to recognize what is already here and open to intuitive sight. God, Divine Mind, the All-in-all, is already here. When we have a clear realization of the Divine Presence, the ideas of the kingdom are made manifest through us, in a form that meets our human needs. First, however, we need to live with a new vision of Spirit, light, and energy. We do not see the true basis of health and of abundant supply, until we look past the illusion of a dead and unyielding world.

Matthew 10:26, Mark 4:22, Luke 8:17, 12:2, and Saying 5 all affirm that nothing is hidden that will not become manifest. This again can be taken on various levels. In one sense, we are heirs to all that is in our Divine Source. The whole spiritual universe is open to us, and is revealed to the degree that we are ready to receive it. In another sense, every pattern of personal thought and belief will become visibly manifest in some form in our everday lives. This is the great law of mental cause and effect.

The Greek text (OP 654, lines 27–31) has an additional phrase at the end of this saying, "nor buried that . . . " Although the last word is missing, it would have been a term meaning the reverse of "buried," namely, "raised." A burial shroud found at Oxyrhynchus records the statement "Jesus says, 'Nothing has been buried that will not be raised.' " This, then, completes the original form of Saying 5b.

Many of the Gnostics did not accept the physical resurrection of Jesus, because their attitude toward the body in general was Puritan or worse, as we would say today. The reason for the Coptic editor's omission is therefore sufficiently clear.

In using the image of burial / resurrection, Jesus touched on basic archetypal themes. He did not mean that physical corpses would be resuscitated on a wide scale. He affirmed, rather, that we all need to die to old limitations of thought and to be reborn into newness of life and understanding. We can, in partnership with our Divine Ground, resurrect buried hopes and aspirations, and fulfill our true purpose and potential in life.

AFFIRMATIONS

—I acknowledge the one Presence, one Power, one Mind in which I live, and move, and have my being.

—The Christ Spirit fills my thoughts with inspiration, and guides my way with infinite wisdom.

—Today I receive Divine guidance. Spirit speaks to me his child; I willingly listen and obey.

—Father-Mother God, you uphold me in my integrity, and set me in Your Presence forever. In communion with your life-giving Spirit, my youth is renewed like the eagle's.

—I trust God to lead me to the place where I can best serve, and where I will be blessed in return with success and prosperity.

---

6. _His disciples questioned him and said to him, "Do you want us to fast? How shall we pray? Shall we give alms? What diet shall we observe?"_

Jesus said, "Do not tell lies, and do not do what you hate, for all things are plain in the sight of heaven. For nothing hidden will not become manifest, and nothing covered will remain without being uncovered." (Nos. 276; 87; 115)

In this dialogue, the disciples ask Jesus about traditional Jewish practices: fasting, prayer, charity, and dietary laws. He does not answer them directly. Instead, he implies that outer observances are of value only to the degree that the motives behind the actions are valid. "Do not tell lies, and do not do what you hate." In effect, then, we are to look to our own inner awareness for what is true, and for determining the nature of right conduct.

The background of this saying is the Book of Tobit in the Apocrypha, where fasting, prayer, and giving alms are praised highly. Jesus' reply, also based on Tobit, alludes to the following verses:

Do not fall into evil ways; for _an honest life_ leads to prosperity. (Tob. 4:6, New English Bible)

Do not do to anyone _what you yourself would hate._ (Tob. 4:15, NEB)

Matthew 6:1–18 summarizes Jesus' policy toward fasting, prayer, and charity. Here also, the motive is far more important than the act itself. All three practices are good, but they are never to be used for the purpose of display. His teaching on these points is to give alms in secret; to commune with the Father silently, in private; and also to fast when it is helpful, but again not to make a show of it. Regarding all three, he declared, "Your Father who sees in secret will reward you" (Matt. 6:4,6,18).

As to dietary laws, Jesus did not strictly follow them. When he instructed the seventy, he said, "Whenever you enter a town and they receive you, eat what is set before you" (Luke 10:8). He totally rejected practices that had no basis in the Torah, but consisted of "traditions of the elders." Mark 7:1–8 gives Jesus' views on the latter. As a rebuke to the Pharisees, he quoted Isaiah 29:13 (as shown in Mark 7:6–7):

> This people honors me with their lips,
> but their heart is far from me;
> In vain do they worship me,
> teaching as doctrines the precepts of men.

"All things are plain in the sight of heaven" may seem out of context. However, reading on in the Book of Isaiah, we find that 29:15 warns,

> Woe to those who hide deep from the Lord their counsel,
> whose deeds are in the dark,
> and who say, "Who sees us? Who knows us?"

This passage states negatively what the close of Saying 6 states positively: "All things are plain in the sight of heaven. For nothing hidden will not become manifest, and nothing covered will remain without being uncovered." Also, the Greek fragment (OP 654, lines 32–39), instead of a word for "heaven," has the Greek *alētheia*, which means "truth." This is the earlier and authentic reading; it also helps to tie the full dialogue together. The term *alētheia* is from the alpha privative (the prefix *a*- meaning "not, the opposite of") and *lanthanō* ("to be hidden," literally or figuratively; "to be ignorant of"; "to forget"). The clear inference of the term is thus that *truth already is;* also, that *it is innately known* by the individual except when hidden or forgotten. Indeed, all things are plain—not hidden or forgotten—in the light of Truth.

AFFIRMATIONS

—In the silence of my inner being, I focus on the living Presence of God. All things are made plain in the light of Truth.

—I am guided in works of charity by the Spirit of God within me. I give and receive of God's bounty in ways that are for the highest good of myself and others.

—My appetite for food and drink are divinely regulated. I am guided to the right foods and beverages, and eat and drink them in the right amounts.

—My periods of abstinence from food and drink are divinely regulated. I am led to the policy that is for my highest good.

---

7. *Jesus said, "Blessed is the lion which becomes man when consumed by man; and cursed is the man whom the lion consumes, and the lion becomes man." (No. 277)*

This saying, in its present form, is disharmonious with itself, for it uses the image of a lion in contradictory ways. The Greek text of Saying 7 (OP 654, lines 40–42) is of little help, being a mere fragment with only a few letters. We can reconstruct the phrase *"ma]kari[os] estin"* (meaning "blessed is") from it, so we know it was a beatitude in form, but that is about as far as it goes.

"Blessed is the lion which becomes man when consumed by man." Revelation 5:5 calls Jesus "the Lion of the tribe of Judah." The first lion of Saying 7 could here refer to Jesus, or to the Indwelling Christ when "consumed" or assimilated by the individual soul.

"Cursed is the man whom the lion consumes, and the lion becomes man." 1 Peter 5:8 warns that "the devil prowls around like a roaring lion, seeking some one to devour." The second lion of Saying 7 could mean collective error when it "consumes" the soul with false beliefs and attitudes.

It is unlikely, however, that Jesus would have used both of these meanings at the same time. He sometimes used paradox, but only where two statements served to point to a larger truth. This does not apply here.

8. *And he said, "The man is like a wise fisherman who cast his net into the sea and drew it up from the sea full of small fish. Among them the wise fisherman found a fine large fish. He threw all the small fish back into the sea and chose the large fish without difficulty. Whoever has ears to hear, let him hear." (Nos. 7, 130)*

This saying is an authentic parable of Jesus. Its imagery is similar to that of the Fish Net (Matt. 13:47–48). The two, however, are separate parables with quite different meanings, and are not based on a single source. Crossan correctly notes that the Parable of the Great Fish is similar in meaning to that of the Hidden Treasure (Matt. 13:44; see also Thom. 109) and the Pearl (Matt. 13:45–46, Thom. 76).

The large fish—as do also the hidden treasure and the pearl—symbolizes the Indwelling Christ, the supreme value in life. The "wise fisherman" accepts the inner kingdom of God, its reality and power. The small fish are lesser values and interests, which he gladly rejects in favor of the "large fish."

Jesus often used the expression "Whoever has ears to hear, let him hear." It is a call to be *spiritually* open and receptive (see Matt. 11:15; 13:9,43; Mark 4:9,23; 7:16—shown only as a footnote in the RSV, thus omitted in Crossan's *Sayings Parallels* on textual grounds—; Luke 8:8; 14:35; Thomas 21, 24, 63, 65, 96).

AFFIRMATIONS

—I am open and receptive to the Mind of Christ.
—I let go all contrary ideas of ignorance, disease, and lack.

—I joyfully accept my Identity in Divine Mind as the supreme value in life.

---

9. *Jesus said, "Now the sower went out, took a handful of seeds, and scattered them. Some fell on the road; the birds came and gathered them up. Others fell on rock, did not take root in the soil, and did not produce ears. And others fell on thorns; they choked the seeds and worms ate them. And others fell on the good soil and it produced good fruit: it bore sixty per measure and a hundred and twenty per measure." (No. 1)*

The Parable of the Sower appears also in Matthew 13:3–9, Mark 4:2–9, and Luke 8:4–8. Its essential teaching is that the kingdom of God is omnipresent and within us, and that it unfolds through the consciousness of the individual. The Sower is here the Indwelling Christ, which is always sowing Divine ideas in the soul.

The four types of ground represent four attitudes that we can take toward this sowing of Divine ideas and guidance. The hard, compacted soil on the road is like a closed mind. The rocky ground, with only a thin layer of soil, is one who has not allowed divine ideas to be established in his or her subconscious mind. The thorny field is one who lets other interests, or negative beliefs, crowd out spiritual progress. The good soil is one who receives Divine ideas gladly, and applies inner guidance in thought, word, and action.

The interpretive comments in Matthew 13:18–23, Mark 4:14–20, and Luke 8:11–15—which are not fully consistent, even among themselves—are conspicuous by their absence. Jesus did not give them. Rather, the early Church added them later because of changing conditions. The Gospel of Thomas omits these commentaries because the original compiler of Thomas did not have them in his sources.

AFFIRMATIONS

—The Sower, the Christ Spirit, fills my thoughts with inspiration and guides my way with infinite wisdom.

—Christ is the head of my life. I am now open, receptive, and obedient to Divine instruction and guidance.

---

10. *Jesus said, "I have cast fire upon the world, and see, I am guarding it until it blazes." (No. 226)*

This saying of Jesus exists in two versions. Luke 12:49 reads, "I came to cast fire upon the earth; and would that it were already kindled!" The difference is that in Thomas it has already been lit. The form in Thomas is more likely to be original. Jesus focused on the living present, whereas the later Church looked more to a future consummation.

Fire is a symbol both of *purification* from what is false, and of *illumination* into spiritual Truth. To cast fire upon the earth also means to transform outer appearances, as fire transmutes wood and straw. Its action in this sense, however, means not to destroy but to renew—as in some natural ecosystems, where a fire renews more than it consumes.

Fire also appears as a symbol of illumination in the biblical account of Pentecost:

And there appeared to them tongues as of fire, distributed and resting on each one of them. And they were all filled with the Holy Spirit and began to speak in other tongues, as the Spirit gave them utterance. (Acts 2:3–4)

According to Matthew 3:11, John the Baptist proclaimed,

I baptize you with water for repentance, but he who is coming after me is mightier than I, whose sandals I am not worthy to carry; he will baptize you with the Holy Spirit and with fire.

AFFIRMATIONS

—The purfying fire of the Holy Spirit works in and through me, cleansing, healing, harmonizing, and adjusting my soul.

—The creative fire of the Holy Spirit inspires me to accomplish great things.

—I am inspired by the Divine Spirit of love, joy, and peace.

—The Indwelling Spirit gives me true understanding, and shows me the way.

---

11. *Jesus said, "This heaven will pass away, and the one above it will pass away. The dead are not alive, and the living will not die. In the days when you consumed what is dead, you made it what is alive. When you come to dwell in the light, what will you do? On the day when you were one you became two. But when you become two, what will you do?" (No. 278)*

"This heaven will pass away, and the one above it will pass away." The biblical version of this saying is closer to the original. It reads, "Heaven and earth will pass away, but my words will not pass away" (Matt. 24:35; Mark 13:31; Luke 21:33). Jesus evidently meant that the race consciousness of this planet *(heaven)*, with its current mixture of truth and error, and of good and evil, will pass away. The *earth*, meaning the resulting mixed conditions on earth, will also be a thing of the past. By contrast, the Divine ideas of the Christ—which Jesus calls *my words*—are eternal and will never pass away. These eternal ideas, one with God, will provide the basis for a transformation of consciousness on our planet. This is the essential meaning of the vision which begins in Revelation 21:1: "Then I saw a new heaven and a new earth; for the first heaven and the first earth had passed away, and the sea was no more."

"The dead are not alive, and the living will not die. In the days when you consumed what is dead, you made it what is alive." The authenticity of this saying is doubtful. It has no supporting evidence. There is, of course, a valid contrast between being spiritually alive and spiritually dead, which Jesus and Paul state in various contexts.

"When you come to dwell in the light, what will you do? On the day when you were one you became two. But when you become two, what will you do?" Jesus used the image of light, and of walking in the light. Also, he may well have contrasted oneness and twoness; if so, the essential contrast was between viewing life according to the Unity of Being, and viewing it in terms of opposites. If this text is based on a saying of Jesus, however, its original form can no longer be determined.

AFFIRMATIONS

—The Indwelling Mind of Christ is now mightily at work to heal all thoughts, beliefs, and outer conditions.

—The solution to every human problem is already worked out in Spirit. I am open and receptive to the answers that are available for me now.

---

12. *The disciples said to Jesus, "We know that you will depart from us. Who is to be our leader?"*

Jesus said to them, "Wherever you are, you are to go to James the righteous, for whose sake heaven and earth came into being."

This saying probably arose among the Jewish Christians in Jerusalem. James the Righteous was Jesus' brother. He became the leader of the Christian community there after the reign of Herod Agrippa (A.D. 41–44). The alleged statement of Jesus, on behalf of James, strengthened the position of the Jerusalem church against contrary claims made on behalf of other Christian factions.

To modern ears, the extravagance of the statement "for whose sake heaven and earth came into being" creates a credibility gap. It did not, however, appear as awkward to the ancient Jews. The Talmud makes the same claim for Abraham, Moses, Aaron, David, and the Messiah.

The decisive point is that Saying 12 is totally contrary to Jesus' teaching as to who should be the greatest among his disciples. These statements show a definite pattern. When his disciples asked who should be first among them, he answered in two ways:

1. Whoever shall be greatest must perform the most service. Their calling was not to be ministered unto, but to minister (Matt. 20:20–28; Mark 10:35–45; Luke 22:24–27).
2. Whoever shall be greatest must become humble and receptive as a child (Matt. 18:1–5; Mark 9:33–37; Luke 9:46–48).

The later Coptic editor added this early (though not authentic) saying, and applied it in a different context. In the second and third centuries, the Naassenes (not the Essenes) claimed to have been the recipients of a secret tradition through James the Righteous. According to them a woman, Mariamne by name, received these traditions from James and later handed them on to the original Naassenes. Saying 12 became—for the Naassenes as well as other dissenting groups—a defense against the growing assumption of authority by "mainstream" church leaders.

13. *Jesus said to his disciples, "Compare me to someone and tell me whom I am like."*

Simon Peter said to him, "You are like a righteous angel."

Matthew said to him, "You are like a wise philosopher."

Thomas said to him, "Master, my mouth is wholly incapable of saying whom you are like."

Jesus said, "I am not your master. Because you have drunk, you have become intoxicated from the bubbling spring which I have measured out."

And he took him and withdrew and told him three things. When Thomas returned to his companions, they asked him, "What did Jesus say to you?"

Thomas said to them, "If I tell you one of the things which he told me, you will pick up stones and throw them at me; a fire will come out of the stones and burn you up." (No. 343)

This dialogue is similar in style to those in Matthew 16:13–20, Mark 8:27–30, and Luke 9:18–21. It is, of course, different in content. The dialogues are similar in that all have Jesus asking his disciples to look beyond surface appearances to know his real inner nature. Thomas is most explicit in pointing to the Christ not only in Jesus, but in the disciples as well.

These dialogues probably record authentic material. In the Gospel of Matthew, Jesus declares, "I tell you, you are Peter, and on this rock I will build my church" (Matt. 16:18). What Jesus, in effect, is doing is giving Simon Bar-Jona (thus called in 16:17) a new name. This signifies a new nature and character, a basic change of consciousness (as *Abram* becoming *Abraham*, and *Jacob* being renamed *Israel*). Jesus could well have meant, then, that Peter— as well as himself—is the Christ and *upon the rock of the Christ in all he would build his ministry.* The belief that Jesus here endowed Peter with temporal authority is a later interpretation.

The pun often noted between "Peter" and "rock" *(petra)* in the Greek language is also in the Aramaic text. The Odes of Solomon, written in a Syriac dialect of Aramaic, express the true meaning of the rock:

> And the foundation of everything is Thy rock.
> And upon it Thou hast built Thy kingdom,
> And it became the dwelling-place of the holy ones.
> (Ode 22:12)

Turning now to the Gospel of Thomas, we find that in Saying 13 Peter and Matthew both missed the subtlety of Jesus' request: "*Compare* me to someone and tell me whom I am *like*." The realm of appearances involves making comparisons and noting contrasts. Christ Consciousness, however, looks beyond duality and paradox and awakens us to the Unity of Being. Therefore, Thomas, by refusing to compare Jesus with anyone else, gave the correct answer. According to the French Coptic scholar, Jean Doresse, his reply in Coptic may be translated as "Master, to whom thou art like, my face [an archetypal image of intellect] fails utterly to grasp."

The fact that the author included this dialogue, which deals with *Thomas's* comments, again points to a Syrian origin for the Gospel of Thomas.

"I am not your master. Because you have drunk, you have become intoxicated from the bubbling spring which I have measured out." Thomas's recognition lifted him above the status of a disciple, and gave him practical equality with Jesus. In mystical language, being drunk can be meant either in a positive or in a negative sense. Here the meaning is clearly positive. The Odes of Solomon, combining the imagery found in Matthew and Thomas, mentions the rock, intoxication, and living water:

> And I was established upon the rock of truth,
> Where He had set me.
> And speaking waters touched my lips
> From the fountain of the Lord generously.
> And so I drank and became intoxicated,
> From the living water that does not die.
> And my intoxication was not with ignorance;
> But I abandoned vanity.
>
> (Ode 11:5–8)

"If I tell you one of the things which he told me, you will pick up stones and throw them at me." This means that the other disciples would have considered his words blasphemous. Death by stoning was the Jewish punishment for blasphemy. When the Pharisees attacked Jesus for calling God his Father, he replied (in John 10:34) by quoting Psalms 82:6:

> I say, "You are gods,
> sons of the Most High, all of you."

(See related Bible passages: Amos 5:21–24; Jer. 2:13; 17:13; John 4:13–14; 7:37–38; 10:31–39; 15:15.)

AFFIRMATIONS

—I have peace like a river in my soul. I accept the peace of God.
—I am inspired by the living waters of Truth.

—I am a son (daughter) of the Living God. I identify with the Cosmic Christ.

---

14. *Jesus said to them, "If you fast, you will give rise to sin for yourselves; and if you pray, you will be condemned; and if you give alms, you will do harm to your spirits. When you go into any land and walk about in the districts, if they receive you, eat what they will set before you, and heal the sick among them. For what goes into your mouth will not defile you, but that which issues from your mouth—it is that which will defile you." (Nos. 106; 147)*

The comments given here regarding fasting, prayer, and charity are contrary to the biblical data, and cannot be accepted as genuine. Jesus' frame of reference does not reject these practices. Rather, it supports them if done in the right spirit, without purposes of display or of demonstrating superiority over others. (Review the commentary on Saying 6.)

Jesus did not, as far as we know, use the formal litanies of the temple. Instead, he spent long periods in close cmmunion with God. Also, he instructed his disciples on meditation and prayer; for example, see Matthew 6:5–15. Practicing his own teaching, he often entered into a meditative state; see Matthew 14:23, 26:36; Mark 1:35, 6:46, 14:32; Luke 6:12, 9:28–29; John 17:1–26.

According to Matthew 4:2 and Luke 4:2, Jesus once fasted for forty days. These sections on the temptations are obviously symbolic. There is, however, no reason to question that he spent an extended period of time without food.

His attitude toward giving alms is reflected in Mark 12:41–44 and Luke 21:1–4. He explained to his disciples that a poor widow, who had given two small copper coins to the temple treasury, had done a greater act than the wealthy who had contributed large sums:

Truly, I say to you, this poor widow has put in more than all those who are contributing to the treasury. For they all contributed out of their abundance; but she out of her poverty has put in everything she had, her whole living. (Mark 12:43–44)

His instructions to "eat what is set before them" and to "heal the sick" are well documented. Luke 10:8–9 records a similar statement, which Jesus made to seventy disciples. Also, the Lucan form treats the healing of the sick as a demonstration of the coming of the kingdom of God:

Whenever you enter a town and they receive you, eat what is set before you; heal the sick in it and say to them, "The kingdom of God has come near to you."

The concluding words of Saying 14 are also authentic, though placed in a somewhat different context than in the canonical gospels. Relevant passages are Matthew 15:10–20 and Mark 7:14–23. For example, Mark 7:15 reads,

There is nothing outside a man which by going into him can defile him; but the things which come out of a man are what defile him.

In the biblical accounts, Jesus makes this statement in support of free choice in the selection of food. This context is reasonable, but the saying should not be taken in too narrow a sense. In a broader way, it affirms that *the inner mind and psyche govern the outer conditions and experiences of one's life.* This affirmation is central to his parables and to the parable genre itself as he used it—implying that life always has two parallel sides, the inner state of consciousness and its outer manifestation.

AFFIRMATIONS

—The foods that I eat are spiritual substance.

—I bless these foods, and give thanks that they nourish my body in wholesome ways.

—I give thanks for the healing energy of Spirit in soul and body. It now works through me to heal myself and others.

---

15. *Jesus said, "When you see one who was not born of woman, prostrate yourselves on your faces and worship him. That one is your father."*

Job 14:1 laments, "Man that is born of a woman is of few days, and full of trouble." This refers to the mortal sense of man, as being subject to sin, sickness, and death. The one *not* born of woman is our eternal Identity, the Christ, which is one with God. Jesus' point here is to worship—to consider the worth of—the Christ in us which is continuous with the Father. This is the Source of healing and illumination, of what Jungians call the process of making whole, or individuation.

Jesus also said, "I and the Father are one" (John 10:30). In the same spirit, Ode 7:7 of Solomon declares,

> The Father of knowledge
> Is the Word of knowledge.

Chapter 1 of the Book of Revelation symbolizes the personal self gaining a vision of the Cosmic Christ. The figure that appears to John in 1:12–16 is not Jesus as he knew him on earth. His is a glorified vision of dominion and power.

Verse 1:17 continues,

When I saw him, I fell at his feet as though dead. But he laid his right hand upon me, saying, "Fear not, I am the first and the last."

When we contact this higher Christ potential, we die to previous limitations of thought. However, our sense of personal identity is not lost. As symbolized by the laying on of the figure's right hand, we are spiritually reborn, empowered, and made whole. Instead of being full of trouble as in Job 14, we are filled with God's peace.

AFFIRMATIONS

—I identify with the Indwelling Christ.
—The Christ is the Word of knowledge, through which the infinite ideas of the kingdom are revealed to me.
—I am empowered through the activity of the Christ in soul and body.
—I now release and express the wholeness that is mine.

---

16. *Jesus said, "Men think, perhaps, that it is peace which I have come to cast upon the world. They do not know that it is dissension which I have come to cast upon the earth: fire, sword, and war. For there will be five in a house: three will be against two, and two against three, the father against the son, and the son against the father. And they will stand solitary." (No. 120)*

Bible students often find statements of this kind troublesome. When attributed to the Prince of Peace, calls for "fire, sword, and war" seem out of character. In his own career, Jesus refused real chances to lead a military revolt against the established order in Palestine. For example, after feeding the multitude, John 6:15 reports,

Perceiving then that they were about to come and take him by force to make him king, Jesus withdrew again to the hills by himself.

Again, when he entered Jerusalem on what is called Palm Sunday, many people proclaimed him king (Matt. 21:9; Mark 11:9–10; Luke 19:38; John 12:13). The word *Hosanna* means "save now"; in its original context, it was a call for political deliverance. Yet he did nothing to carry out their wishes.

Just the same, however, Matthew 10:34–36 and Luke 12:51–53 contain material similar to Thomas 16. Thus, sayings of this kind were part of the oral tradition at an early date. We have two choices. Either we can conclude that these sayings are false, or we can look for a frame of reference in which they are congruous with Jesus' words and actions as a whole.

In one sense, Jesus' statements could have served as a warning. They were not intended to provoke civic unrest. Rather, he would have reminded his disciples that the transition from the old order to the new would be upsetting and difficult. The needed paradigm shift would not be smooth, even if his followers avoided worldly weapons and methods. Resistance would occur to the rule of love and truth on earth, families would be divided, and old institutions would fall.

Again, on the level of archetypal imagery, a sword sometimes represents the Logos, Word, or Indwelling Christ, slaying what is false and negative in the soul. For example, Hebrews 4:12 declares,

For the word *[logos]* of God is living and active, sharper than any two-edged sword, piercing to the division of soul and spirit, of joints and marrow, and discerning the thoughts and intentions of the heart.

Paul's self-image as a spiritual warrior is reflected in his allegory in Ephesians 6:10–17. He concludes it. "And take the helmet of salvation, and the sword of the Spirit, which is the word of God" (Eph. 6:17).

Matthew Black's research adds clarity to a related verse. The Revised Standard Version translates Matthew 10:34: "Do not think that I have come to bring peace on earth; I have not come to bring peace, but a sword." The Old Syriac, however, is translated: "I have not come to set peace on earth, but *divisions of minds* and a sword!"[1] This means that truth and falsehood (as in Hebrews 4:12) must be separated in the psyche. There can be no peace between the real and the counterfeit. The real must "win" and reduce the unreal to its native nothingness. This is done through a spiritual sword, the active Word of God within.

Apparently, then, the "fire, sword, and war" in Thomas refer to inner conflicts that must be resolved before complete wholeness can appear. The following are to be slain by the sword of Truth: hate, fear, anger, envy, greed, wrongdoing, and false habits of every kind.

Coptic scholars differ on the translation of the ending of Thomas 16. "They will stand solitary" can also be translated, "They will stand because they are single ones" (according to William R. Schoedel). To a nonspecialist, at least, the latter translation makes more sense. To be solitary means to be alone and separate; but it is precisely this sense of isolation that the Gospel of Thomas seeks to overcome. Even when one "stands alone" for a principle, it should not be as a sullen outsider, with self-righteous scorn. To stand alone in a positive, Christian sense is to be attuned with the spiritual universe on some point, even when others are out of tune. It is the sustained ability to realize oneness and truth when others see only separation and error.

To be *single*, of course, does not refer to one's marital status. It means to be totally attuned to God, to Divine Mind, to the Indwelling Christ. The single ones are safe in all situations. They are attuned to what is good, whole, and true.

AFFIRMATIONS

—I am attuned to the one Presence, one Mind, one Power that is all.

—The Word of Truth establishes its wisdom, love, beauty, and harmony within my soul and body.

—I let go of all error and negative thinking. I am renewed in the spirit of my mind.

17. *Jesus said, "I shall give you what no eye has seen and what no ear has heard and what no hand has touched and what has never occurred to the human mind." (No. 246)*

The author of Thomas took this saying from an unknown writing, from which Paul also quoted. Paul, however, makes no reference to Jesus as its source. Also, he omits the phrase, "what no hand has touched."

But, as it is written,

"What no eye has seen, nor ear heard,
nor the heart of man conceived,
what God has prepared for those who love him,"

God has revealed to us through the Spirit. For the Spirit
searches everything, even the depths of God. (1 Cor. 2:9–10)

There is no evidence that Jesus *wrote* anything, except for a few unknown words on the ground in John 8:6. He taught through the spoken word, works of power that demonstrated the truth of his teachings, and parables of action. Thus not Jesus, but another Jew (who need not have been Christian) wrote this lost work. Thomas 17 and 1 Corinthians 2:9 expand the meaning of Isaiah 64:4, which reads,

From of old no one has heard
or perceived by the ear,
no eye has seen a God besides thee,
who works for those who wait for him.

We are reminded, then, that God illumines us in a way that eye has not seen, nor ear heard, nor hand touched. Also, our loving Creator has *already* prepared for the supply of every human need.

AFFIRMATIONS

—I give thanks for the supply of every need, both invisible and visible.
—I give thanks for the Indwelling Love that God is, now working its will in and through me.
—In the silence of my spirit, I wait for God to reveal his nature and purpose.

---

18. *The disciples said to Jesus, "Tell us how our end will be."*
Jesus said, "Have you discovered, then, the beginning, that you look for the end? For where the beginning is, there will the end be. Blessed is he who will take his place in the beginning; he will know the end and will not experience death."

In common with many great mystics, both Christian and non-Christian, Jesus had a direct experience of eternity that transcends the human sense of time and space. He thus affirms that in Divine Mind, the beginning and the end are the same. The Jewish mystics used the term Elohim, as in Genesis 1:1–2:3. In the Christian perspective, the beginning and the consummation of our existence converge in our spiritual Identity, the "I AM" or Cosmic Christ that is one with God. Christ was our origin, and is now our sustaining Identity; moreover, our eternal destiny is to fully show forth the Christ nature and power. As Paul affirmed, "For *from* him and *through* him and *to* him are all things. To him be glory for ever" (Rom. 11:36).

The Odes of Solomon declare,

> From the beginning until the end
> I received His knowledge.
>
> (Ode 11:4)

The Odes also use "the place" in a symbolic sense—as does John 14:2–3—meaning a consciousness of eternal life:

> I went up into the light of Truth as into a chariot,
> And the Truth led me and caused me to come . . . .
> And became for me a haven of salvation,
> And set me on *the place* of immortal life.
>
> (Ode 38:1,3)

The Book of Revelation makes the same basic affirmation as Saying 18 (*alpha* and *omega* are the first and last letters of the Greek alphabet, respectively):

"I am the Alpha and the Omega," says the Lord God, who is and who was and who is to come, the Almighty [in Greek, *Pantokratōr, The All-governing*]. (Rev. 1:8)

I am the Alpha and the Omega, the beginning and the end. To the thirsty I will give water without price from the fountain of the water of life. He who conquers shall have this heritage, and I will be his God and he shall be my son. (Rev. 21:6–7)

AFFIRMATIONS

—I attune myself to the I AM, Elohim, the Cosmic Christ.

—I am one with the All-governing Presence of Good, the one Energy that is all-sufficient in all things.

—From this inmost Center of my being, I show forth whatever I need: health, abundance, protection, and harmony in all my experiences, conditions, and affairs.

---

19. *Jesus said, "Blessed is he who came into being before he came into being. If you become my disciples and listen to my words, these stones will minister to you.*

For there are five trees for you in Paradise which remain undisturbed summer and winter and whose leaves do not fall. Whoever becomes acquainted with them will not experience death."

"Blessed is he who came into being before he came into being." Two other sources also attribute this saying to Jesus. Irenaeus, Bishop of Lyons, quotes it as follows: "Blessed is he who was before becoming man." The Gospel of Philip, also found at Nag Hammadi, reads, "The Lord said, 'Blessed is he who is before he came into being. For he who is, has been and shall be.' "

Probably an authentic saying, it affirms the preexistence of the "I AM," and also—in a derived sense—the certainty of the soul's continuation in eternal life. Jesus made the same point in John 8:58: "Before Abraham was, I am." He meant, "Blessed are they who know their true Identity, which is changeless and indestructible."

"If you become my disciples and listen to my words, these stones will minister to you." This affirms the continuity between the inner thought and the outer picture on earth. The formative power of thought is a basic law of the universe. It is similar in meaning to John 15:7–8:

If you abide in me, and my words abide in you, ask whatever you will, and it shall be done for you. By this my Father is glorified, that you bear much fruit, and so prove to be my disciples.

The five trees in Paradise point to the potential for transcending the five physical senses. They refer to the intuitive faculties, of which ordinary sight, hearing, smell, taste, and touch are the symbols. Much as we learned to use our bodily senses by practice, so also we can learn to use our spiritual senses. Jesus made a similar point in the Parable of the Ten Virgins (Matt. 25:1–10; see Thomas 75). The five wise girls (spiritual faculties) are accepted into the wedding feast, while the five foolish girls (physical senses) are shut out. In the world of Jesus' parable, they are admitted to the wedding feast because they sense the unseen realm of causes. Through their functioning, we are consciously united to God, the All-in-all.

AFFIRMATIONS

—I relax, and turn to the realm of infinite ideas in which I live, move, and have my being.

—I am grounded in the eternal Mind of Christ.

—I listen to the Indwelling Spirit, and attune to Spirit's action in thought, word, and deed.

—I align my consciousness with the power and dominion of the Indwelling Christ.

20. *The disciples said to Jesus, "Tell us what the kingdom of heaven is like."*

He said to them, "It is like a mustard seed. It is the smallest of all seeds. But when it falls on tilled soil, it produces a great plant and becomes a shelter for birds of the sky." (No. 3)

The Parable of the Mustard Seed also appears in Matthew 13:31–32, Mark 4:30–32, and Luke 13:18–19. It gives a dramatic picture of the power of increase. Just so can spiritual consciousness increase in the soul. It begins as a tiny seed in the mind, but continues to expand until it becomes completely dominant.

Another of Jesus' sayings about the mustard seed emphasizes the active power of faith. It is a variation of the basic teaching "As within, so without":

If you have faith as a grain of mustard seed, you will say to this mountain, "Move from here to there," and it will move; and nothing will be impossible to you. (Matt. 17:20; see also Luke 17:6)

AFFIRMATIONS

—As I attune to the Omnipresence of God, the reality of that Presence becomes more and more clear to me.

—My inner faith is quickened, as I think of my highest understanding of Truth.

—This quickened faith is released through me to accomplish every good thing.

---

21. *Mary said to Jesus, "Whom are your disciples like?"*

He said, "They are like children who have settled in a field which is not theirs. When the owners of the field come, they will say, 'Let us have back our field.' They (will) undress in their presence in order to let them have back their field and to give it back to them. Therefore I say, if the owner of a house knows that the thief is coming, he will begin his vigil before he comes and will not let him dig through into his house of his domain to carry away his goods. (No. 206) You, then, be on your guard against the world. Arm yourselves with great strength lest the robbers find a way to come to you, for the difficulty which you expect will (surely) materialize. Let there be among you a man of understanding. When the grain ripened, he came quickly with his sickle in his hand and reaped it. (No. 16) Whoever has ears to hear, let him hear." (No. 130)

It is uncertain whether the Children in the Field is an authentic parable of Jesus. His parables, except for an occasional use of hyperbole or parody to make a point, were true to life. Normally, children would not be allowed to settle in a field apart from their parents. He could, however, have referred to groups of homeless, vagrant children who subsisted on the fringes of society.

Again, while children might take off their clothes, they would not do so *because* they were being chased off someone's field. They would just make a run for it. Perhaps this is the parody used here to make a point. Putting off an old garmet, and putting on a new one, represents a basic change in one's belief system and way of life. Jesus used this imagery in his parables. He advised against sewing a new patch on an old garment (Matt. 9:16; Mark 2:21; Luke 5:36) or an old patch on a new one (Thomas 47). It is better to discard the old garment entirely, and henceforth to wear a new one. Also, we are not to enter the marriage feast without a wedding garment (Matt. 22:11-13). The Prodigal Son, when he returned to his father's house, received a new robe (Luke 15:22).

Four versions of the Simile of the Burglar exist. These are found in Thomas 21 and 103, Matthew 24:43, and Luke 12:39. As its original context is uncertain, it is difficult to interpret. Perhaps Jesus meant the thief as a symbol of collective error, a danger to be avoided. In Matthew and Luke, the burglar is related to the appearance of the "Son of Man." This analogy is unlikely, and reflects a later view of things that developed *after* Jesus' death and resurrection. Thomas 21 relates it to the story of the children in the field, though the connection is weak and contrived. Thomas 103 gives no setting whatever.

In Thomas 21, the simile is followed by the warning "You, then, be on your guard against the world. Arm yourselves with great strength lest the robbers find a way to come to you, for the difficulty which you expect will (surely) materialize." If the Coptic editor viewed the earth plane in a negative and hostile way, this accords well with his beliefs.

However, it is possible that the connection is original. If so, Jesus intended to *parody* a negative and defensive attitude toward life—to make light of it, so to speak. If he intended satire, he framed it well, for "the difficulty which you expect will surely materialize" fits as an ironic paraphrase of Job 3:25:

> For the thing that I fear comes upon me,
> and what I dread befalls me.

Our Egyptian editor, however, would have missed the point.

"Let there be among you a man of understanding." If "among you" is taken to mean "within your own consciousness(es)," this saying has much to commend it. The Indwelling Christ is the "man of understanding" that we need to make conscious among us. It is our true Selfhood, and the Source of our individual and collective well-being. When we are attuned to our spiritual inheritance, we are true to ourselves and in harmony with one another.

The reference to the reaper is based on Joel 3:13. It also concludes Jesus' Parable of the Seed Growing Secretly, in Mark 4:26-29. Verse 29 reads, "But when the grain is ripe, at once he puts in the sickle, because the harvest has come." This has an important message: there is a right time to accept God-given opportunities as they appear in life. The simile, as Jesus uses it, relates to the timeliness of a farmer in harvesting a field of grain. If reaped too soon, it may have too much moisture and rot in storage. If the farmer waits too long, a storm or other severe weather may damage or destroy the crop. It is well to affirm in meditation: "I am in the right place at the right time." There is no time in Spirit, but there is an orderly sequence by which blessings and opportunities unfold.

"Whoever has ears to hear, let him hear." As stated in the commentary on Saying 8, Jesus often said this as a call to be spiritually open and receptive.

AFFIRMATIONS

—I attune myself to the Indwelling Christ, the Man of Understanding. I am that True Man. It is awakened in my own consciousness and in that of others.

—I am alert to opportunities that are in Divine Order for me.

—I am always in the right place at the right time, because God is in charge of my life and affairs.

---

22. *Jesus saw infants being suckled. He said to his disciples, "These infants being suckled are like those who enter the kingdom." (No. 158)*

They said to Him, "Shall we then, as children, enter the kingdom?"

Jesus said to them, "When you make the two one, and when you make the inside like the outside and the outside like the inside, and the above like the below, and when you make the male and the female one and the same, so that the male not be male nor the female female; and when you fashion eyes in place of an eye, and a hand in place of a hand, and a foot in place of a foot, and a likeness in place of a likeness; then will you enter [the kingdom]." (No. 377)

"These infants being suckled are like those who enter the kingdom." As a infant suckling milk, those who enter the kingdom do so willingly and without any argument or debate. Jesus, as well as others of the first century, used similar analogies. He said, for example, that his disciples must become like children in order to enter the kingdom (Matt. 18:1–4). Also consider his well-known statement to Nicodemus: "Truly, truly, I say to you, unless one is born anew, he cannot see the kingdom of God" (John 3:3). In addition, Paul used milk as a metaphor for teachings to be given to novices on the spiritual path; that is, "babes in Christ" (1 Cor. 3:1–2).

1 Peter 2:2–3 declares,

Like newborn babes, long for the pure spiritual milk, that by it you may grow up to salvation; for you have tasted the kindness of the Lord.

According to the Odes of Solomon 8:14,

> I fashioned their members,
> And my own breasts I prepared for them,
> That they might drink my holy milk and live by it.

The second part of Saying 22 features four contrasts:

> two / one
> inside / outside
> above / below
> male / female

These contrasts are open-ended, in that they allow for various shades of meaning and are intended to do so. They open the mind to new insights as the reader interacts with them. That they are largely authentic is supported by other early documents. 2 Clement, the Gospel of the Egyptians, the Gospel of Philip, and the Martyrdom of Peter all include some of them, drawing from oral tradition. Even the Acts of Thomas, a third-century Syrian work, reads,

Him that was inward have I made outward, and the outward inward, and all thy fullness hath been fulfilled in me. (Acts of Thomas 147)

TWO / ONE.

Making the two one suggests that the Divine will and the human will are to be harmonized. Thoughts of conflict give way to the realization of Oneness. Also, inner conflicts are resolved. The mind and the heart, logic and intuition, are reconciled from a higher level. Our thoughts and our feelings work in the same direction, not at cross-purposes. In addition, the mind is lifted above the human sense of opposites, and is unified with the Cosmic Christ.

INSIDE / OUTSIDE.

Plato declared, "May the inner man and the outer man become one." Jesus warned,

Woe to you, scribes and Pharisees, hypocrites! for you cleanse the outside of the cup and of the plate, but inside they are full of extortion and rapacity. You blind Pharisee! first cleanse the inside of the cup and of the plate, that the outside also may be clean. (Matt. 23:25–26)

2 Clement 12:4 reads, "And by 'the outside as the inside' he means this, that the inside is the soul, and the outside is the body."
These statements about the inside and the outside are especially rich in the variety of meanings that they suggest. They reflect the basic truth that the inner consciousness governs the outer picture of things.

ABOVE / BELOW.

This pair again affirms that causation is mental, not physical. In esoteric writings, above=within, and below=without. The Odes of Solomon 34:4–5 gives an excellent example of this teaching:

> The likeness of that which is below
> Is that which is above.
> For everything is from above,
> And from below there is nothing,
> But it is believed to be by those in whom
> there is no understanding.

MALE / FEMALE.

To "make the male and female one and the same" can be interpreted on several levels. In one sense, it is a mandate for members of both sexes to enjoy equal rights, equal opportunities, and equal respect. In a similar way, Paul declared:

There is neither Jew nor Greek, there is neither slave nor free, there is neither male nor female; for you are all one in Christ Jesus. (Gal. 3:28)

In addition, Jesus sought to reconcile the "male" and the "female" within the individual soul. Thought and feeling, the objective and the subjective, the conscious and the subconscious, were to be balanced and harmonized.

Pachomius and his followers may have added yet another meaning: To renounce marriage and, in so doing, to avoid conjugal relations.

The third part of Saying 22 can best be shown as poetry:

> When you fashion eyes in place of an eye,
> and a hand in place of a hand,
> and a foot in place of a foot,
> and a likeness in place of a likeness;
> then will you enter the kingdom.

Jesus uses similar imagery of the eye, the hand, and the foot in Matthew 5:29–30, 18:8–9, and Mark 9:43–47. As shown in the Bible, Jesus often used Aramaic idioms to make his point. In the related biblical symbology, we are told to cast off attitudes that project evil on others, which could lead us to violate their rights. George Lamsa informs us,

"Cut off your hand and pluck out your eye" is an Eastern idiom meaning "stop stealing, stop envying." "Cut off your foot" means, "Do not trespass in another man's field or vineyard." . . . . What Jesus meant here was the destruction of the habit of stealing, envying and trespassing, rather than the destruction of members of the body, for members of the body are the agents of the mind.[1]

The quotation in Thomas brings out the positive side. The *new eyes* refer to an intuitive way of seeing. We awaken to the omnipresence of God, and give up bondage to our limiting beliefs about life. We look beyond the outer appearance of flesh and bones to the realm of causes. *The new hand* is a new way of working and achieving goals. We correct our thoughts, beliefs, images, and attitudes, instead of working to change only our surroundings. *The new foot* is a restored understanding. We let go of a false belief system, and welcome the intuitive knowledge of the Unity of Being. *The new likeness* means the likeness of God, as we show it forth in thought, word, and action.

AFFIRMATIONS

—I am ready to put aside human pride, and to receive fresh understanding. The Holy Spirit is my teacher; I listen and obey.

—I am willing to see life as One. I am willing to let the Christ Mind move into my awareness, and make soul and body whole.

—I am willing to let the peace, order, and harmony of Spirit move in and through me, and outward into my world.

—I am willing for the greater Mind of Spirit to unify my thoughts and feelings according to Its own Truth.

—I am willing to see the earth in a new way; to be empowered through the inner Law of my being; to awaken to my true Self, which is one with God.

---

23. *Jesus said, "I shall choose you, one out of a thousand, and two out of ten thousand, and they shall stand as a single one."*

In Matthew 22:14, Jesus declared, "Many are called, but few are chosen." Evidently, then, to be *called* means one thing, and to be *chosen* means something else. The call to live in tune with the Infinite, though made to many, was taken up in earnest by few.

Some of Koheleth's sayings—in the Old Testament Book of Ecclesiastes—seem to be the product of a hardened cynic. For example,

One man among a thousand I found, but a woman among all these I have not found. Behold, this alone I found, that God made man upright, but they have sought out many devices. (Eccles. 7:28–29)

This reminds one of Diogenes' proverbial search for an honest man.

Jesus, however, did not mean Saying 23 cynically. His emphasis is not on the many who have fallen short, but on the two out of 10,000 who "shall stand as a single one." It is a message of hope, meaning that a few meditators can "stand as a single one" and bring forth better conditions on earth. This does not remove the need for outer action, but it can give such action the direction that it needs. If only a small minority of people began meditating regularly on the great truths of God, it would be enough to bring an all-around improvement to society. Health, joy, and prosperity would increase, and the moral climate would greatly improve. To a substantial degree, this is already taking place.

AFFIRMATIONS

—Let liberty, justice, and peace reign in the minds and hearts of all people everywhere.

—Let the love and peace that the Christ gives now reign within all people everywhere.

—I (we) affirm the unifying of all souls in the order and harmony of Spirit.

---

24. *His disciples said to him, "Show us the place where you are, since it is necessary for us to seek it."*

He said to them, "Whoever has ears, let him hear. There is light within a man of light, and he lights up the whole world. If he does not shine, he is darkness." (Nos. 45, 130)

The disciples' question is similar to that of Philip in John 14:8: "Lord, show us the Father, and we shall be satisfied" (see John 13:36, 14:5). Again, we can see that "the place" refers to a state of consciousness. The disciples strongly desired this inner awareness, and wanted to know how to reach it.

From great antiquity, light has been an archetypal image of the Divine. And in his reply Jesus reminded them of their own inner Being, of *the Divine Light that is within them.* What they sought was already present, waiting to be discovered and released into expression.

According to John 14:5–6,

Thomas said to him, "Lord, we do not know where you are going; how can we know the way?" Jesus said to him, "I am the way, and the truth, and the life; no one comes to the Father, but by me."

On the surface, this may appear to contradict Saying 24 in Thomas, but it does not. In John 14:6, Jesus meant that the *I AM* or *Indwelling Christ* is the way, the truth, and the life. Only through the I AM can one know the Father. The two sources are really saying the same thing in different words.

The theme of light and darkness, of course, is a prominent one in the Essene literature, the Gospel of John, and the Odes of Solomon. The answer attributed to Jesus in Thomas 24 is entirely plausible. Both inward illumination, and the luminosity of the body and of the earth—although not ordinarily seen in this way—are real. The light has a healing connotation as well. Jesus also said,

Your eye is the lamp of your body; when your eye is sound [KJV—single], your whole body is full of light; but when it is not sound, your body is full of darkness. Therefore be careful lest the light in you be darkness. If then your whole body is full of light, having no part dark, it will be wholly bright, as when a lamp with its rays gives you light. (Luke 11:34–36; see also Matt. 6:22– 23)

AFFIRMATIONS

—I relax, and realize the Inner Light of the Christ.

—I am the light of the world. I show forth the bright, shining light of the Indwelling God.

—I identify with the Inner Light, and move and have my being within It.

— Through the Inner Light, I am healed, harmonized, and made whole.

---

25. *Jesus said, "Love your brother like your soul, guard him like the pupil of your eye."*

This authentic saying of Jesus gets to the heart of applied Christianity. If we love others by beholding the Christ in them, we will also know the Christ in ourselves with clarity. In a consciousness of oneness, we then gain a deeper sense of the call to "love your neighbor as yourself" (Lev. 19:18).

The pupil of the eye also appears in the Old Testament. For example, Deuteronomy 32:10 proclaims God's love for Israel:

> He found him in a desert land,
> and in the howling waste of the wilderness;
> he encircled him, he cared for him,
> he kept him as the apple of his eye.

Jesus wanted his disciples to be clear channels for Divine Love to function through them. Both Clement of Alexandria and Tertullian record the following saying of Jesus, taken from oral tradition: "You have seen your brother; you have seen your God."

AFFIRMATIONS

—I am awake to the indwelling reality of God, which is Universal Love.

—I am a clear channel for Divine Love working through me.

—Realizing that God is All, I love God with my whole heart, and soul, and mind, and strength. I love my neighbor, and I love myself, as we are all in and of God.

Also: Read Deuteronomy 6:4–5, Matthew 22:34–40, Mark 12:28–34,

Luke 10:25–28, John 13:34–35 and 15:12–17, 1 Corinthians 13, and 1 John 4:7–21.

---

26. *Jesus said, "You see the mote in your brother's eye, but you do not see the beam in your own eye. When you cast the beam out of your own eye, then you will see clearly to cast the mote from your brother's eye." (No. 83)*

This saying also appears in Matthew 7:3–5 and Luke 6:41–42. Its Greek and Coptic versions in Thomas essentially agree. In subject matter, it connects with Saying 25, which has to do with loving one another.

Jesus here raises an essential point of his teaching: in order to truly love one another, we must overcome the tendency to project our own negativity on others. In the same context, Matthew 7:1–2 warns,

Judge not, that you be not judged. For with the judgment you pronounce you will be judged, and the measure you give will be the measure you get.

The teaching is positive in that we *can* cast the beam out of our own soul, so that we can be truly useful in helping others to do so. To cast out the beam, however, requires a basic change in mental and emotional direction. In fact, it requires total forgiveness of self and others. By finding our spiritual Identity, the Christ, we also find that our brother's true Identity is the same as our own.

AFFIRMATIONS

—There is one universal Christ Mind, which indwells all and sustains all.

—I behold the Christ in you, as I also behold the Christ in myself.

—Divine Love is now released in and through me (you), to do its perfect work.

---

27. *Jesus said, "If you do not fast as regards the world, you will not find the kingdom. If you do not observe the Sabbath as a Sabbath, you will not see the father." (No. 287)*

These are authentic teachings of Jesus, supported by other extracanonical sources. Clement of Alexandria quoted the first half of Saying 27 as a beatitude: "Blessed are those who fast to the world." A spiritual fast is also called for in The Shepherd of Hermas (early second century A.D.). For example, Similitude 5:5 reads,

The true fast is this: Do nothing wickedly in your life, but serve God with a pure mind; and keep his commandments and walk according to his precepts, nor let any wicked desire to enter the mind.

Jesus enlarged on, but did not originate, the spiritual meaning of fasting. The Book of Isaiah gives fasting a dual meaning: on one level, it is becoming free of perceptual errors and negative emotional states. In another sense, it refers to establishing justice and to helping those in need:

> Is not this the fast that I choose:
> to loose the bonds of wickedness,
> to undo the thongs of the yoke,
> to let the oppressed go free,
> and to break every yoke?
> Is it not to share your bread with the hungry,
> and bring the homeless poor into your house;
> when you see the naked, to cover him,
> and not to hide yourself from your own flesh?
> Then shall your light break forth like the dawn,
> and your healing shall spring up speedily;
> your righteousness shall go before you,
> the glory of the Lord shall be your rear guard.
> (Isa. 58:6–8)

In Thomas, in order to find the kingdom ("kingdom of God" in the Greek text, OP 1, lines 4–11), we need to fast to the world. This does not mean to become a monk, as many in the early Church came to believe. It means to fast from worldly thinking, to reject a false and limited sense of life based on the illusion of God's absence. Only by letting go of an egoistic frame of reference can we become conscious members of the kingdom of Divine life, truth, and love.

"Keeping the Sabbath as a Sabbath" is mentioned by Tertullian and by Justin Martyr. Justin states, "The new law requires you to keep a perpetual Sabbath." This does not rule out the practice of resting and worshiping one day in seven—still an excellent idea. Nor does it tell us to be idlers who do no work. It means that whatever we are doing, we are to remain open and receptive to the action of God in mind, body, and affairs. Ephesians 6:13 advises, "Having done all, to stand." There is a time when we need to cease human concern, and to let go and let God do His perfect work.

We sabbatize all of life when we inwardly rest in the Divine Presence, in every activity and in all situations.

AFFIRMATIONS

—I mentally fast from all that is false; I think on all that is true of God's Omnipresence.

—I mentally fast from all that is evil; I think on all that is good.

—I mentally fast from all belief in disease; I celebrate Spirit's wholeness in myself and others.

—I mentally fast from all belief in lack; I celebrate Spirit's abundant supply in my life and in that of others.

—I mentally fast from all belief in conflict; I celebrate Spirit's love and harmony in my life and in that of others.

—I release all personal concern; I accept the peace of God.

—I let the Divine Presence complete Its perfect work in, through, and around me now.

---

28. *Jesus said, "I took my place in the midst of the world, and I appeared to them in flesh. I found all of them intoxicated; I found none of them thirsty. And my soul became afflicted for the sons of men, because they are blind in their hearts and do not have sight; for empty they came into the world, and empty too they seek to leave the world. But for the moment they are intoxicated. When they shake off their wine, then they will repent."*

This is a vivid set of images, which were not unusual for their time. For example, being drunk often represented spiritual ignorance on some level, as in Luke 21:34, 1 Thessalonians 5:6–8, and 1 Corinthians 15:32–34 (although being drunk with wine is not excluded). The Odes of Solomon, using similar imagery, contrasts the light of Truth with deceit and error:

> And I asked the Truth, Who are these?
> And He said to me: This is the Deceiver and the Error.
> And they imitate the Beloved and His Bride,
> And they cause the world to err and corrupt it.
> And they invite many to the wedding feast,
> And allow them to drink the wine of their intoxication;
> So they cause them to vomit up their wisdom and their knowledge,
> And make them senseless.
>
> (Ode 38:10–13)

The Hermetic writings of Egypt contain similar language. For example, the Poimandres—which means "Shepherd of Men"!— declares,

> O peoples, earthborn men, who have given yourselves over to drunkenness and sleep and ignorance of God, cease revelling under the enchantment of irrational sleep .... Depart from the light which is darkness. (Corpus Hermeticum I, 27)

The Greek text of Thomas (OP 1, lines 11– 22) is here broken off, and we do not have the final 40 percent of this saying in Greek. The Coptic translation, however, includes the Greek loan word *metanoia* at the end. This is the same word that is translated "repentance" in the English New Testament. *Metanoia* refers to a basic change in consciousness, for the term means "a change of the mind; a change of the inner man." It derives, in turn, from *meta-* (beyond) and *nous* (the reasoning mind). *Metanoia*, then, means not only a new direction of thought, but also illumination into a higher order of understanding, beyond human reasoning and logic. This is the awakening to which Jesus still calls us today.

—I receive the Divine Light that dissolves all darkness.

—I awaken to the Divine Wisdom that dissolves the false belief in ignorance.

—I invite the action of the Indwelling Christ, which establishes Its own wholeness, harmony, and energy in my soul.

---

29. *Jesus said, "If the flesh came into being because of spirit, it is a wonder. But if spirit came into being because of the body, it is a wonder of wonders. Indeed, I am amazed at how this great wealth has made its home in this poverty."*

Saying 29 contrasts the images of spirit/flesh and wealth/poverty. Given the biases of the Coptic editor, its text has certainly been distorted. The reverse side of OP 1 includes a fragment of this saying. Only parts of two words, remain, however, so it is of little help in determining the earlier, Greek wording.

If this is based on a true saying of Jesus, the original would have affirmed, in some form, that the visible world does not explain itself. It depends for its existence, and for its day-to-day functioning, on the Omnipresent Spirit that we call God. Also, to focus on Divine ideas is true wealth, and brings abundant living into expression. But to focus only on the external world is to dwell on lack and limitation, which amounts to poverty.

Hebrews 11:3 affirms,

By faith we understand that the world was created by the word of God, so that what is seen was made out of things which do not appear.

30. *Jesus said, "Where there are three gods, they are gods. Where there are two or one, I am with him." (No. 166)*

This is a corrupted version of an original saying. It had to do with the energy released when two or more people combine their spiritual focus. It also pointed to the omnipresence of God, not to three gods, as the Source of power. The same saying in the Greek edition (OP 1, lines 24–31) is partially worn away. Considering the gaps in OP 1—and here one may differ with part of Crossan's reconstruction—its probable original sense is

Where there are [two—see Thom. 23], they are [not—filling a gap] without God; and where there is but [a single one], I say that I am with [him]. Lift up the stone, and you will find me there. Split the piece of wood, and I am there.

The Coptic editor took the second statement about the stone and the wood, changed the wood and the stone to the reverse order, and attached it to Saying 77. This again shows that he reworked the text wherever he saw fit to do so.

The authors of Matthew and Thomas drew on similar traditions here. Matthew 18:18–20 reads,

¹⁸Truly, I say to you, whatever you bind on earth shall be bound [future perfect tense—"shall have been bound"] in heaven, and whatever you loose on earth shall be loosed [future perfect tense—"shall have been loosed"] in heaven. ¹⁹Again, I say to you, if two of you agree on earth about anything they ask, it will be done for them by my Father in heaven. ²⁰For where two or three are gathered in my name, there am I in the midst of them.

"Heaven" here means the inward consciousness, and "earth" the visible results. The Greek verbs for "bind" and "loose," being in their future perfect form, are a strong affirmation of the formative power of thought. Whatever is bound or loosed in the earth (the outer appearance) must first have been bound or loosed in heaven (the inner realms of thought). The inner controls the outer. Thus we find that Matthew 18:18 and 18:19–20 fit together well. Also, there is a good possibility that Jesus gave the statement about the stone and the wood on the same occasion.

"The agreement of two" can convey more than one level of meaning. One is the obvious; that is, two people meditating or visualizing in unison. Another sense is that the *thought* plus the *feeling* of one individual, when brought into agreement, is sufficient to release the power of the God within. Both are correct, and both are part of the teaching that Jesus presented to his disciples.

AFFIRMATIONS

—The Indwelling Christ is ever at work within me, to heal my thoughts and my feelings. Both work in unison to bring forth the glory of God through me.

—All people and things dwell in, and are sustained by, the One Divine Spirit: people, animals, plants, minerals, everything.

—Therefore, the Divine Spirit is in absolute control, and that Spirit works only for good.

—Through the all-governing Mind of Christ, I claim my good now.

---

31. *Jesus said, "No prophet is accepted in his own village; no physician heals those who know him." (No. 146)*

The full saying fits the pattern of Jesus' actions. That is to say, in his ministry he combined the functions of a prophet and a healer. The meaning of the Greek text of Thomas (OP 1, lines 31–36) is substantially the same. And, in the Synoptic Gospels, the setting is his return to his home town of Nazareth (Mark 6:4; see also Matt. 13:57; Luke 4:23–24). Finally, John 4:44 reads, "Jesus himself testified that a prophet has no honor in his own country."

"No physician heals those who know him." This is not literally true, but it made sense in the context of the times. In the first century, many healers in the eastern Mediterranean area traveled widely. Their power of suggestion, which contributed greatly to the healing of patients, lay largely in the fact that their public was not overly familiar with them. In Jesus' case, the townspeople had known him since early childhood. He had, like other little children, played in the streets, gotten his face dirty, and made a certain amount of mischief. This tended to disqualify him as a healer and prophet in their own eyes, though his public strongly acclaimed him a few miles from home.

32. *Jesus said, "A city being built on a high mountain and fortified cannot fall, nor can it be hidden." (No. 46)*

This saying of Jesus has its literary background in Isaiah 2:2:

> It shall come to pass in the latter days
> that the mountain of the house of the Lord
> shall be established as the highest of the mountains,
> and shall be raised above the hills;
> and all the nations shall flow to it.

Isaiah's archetypal imagery—including the mountain and the house of the Lord—points above all to inner illumination. Matthew 5:14 is similar to Thomas 32: "You are the light of the world. A city set on a hill cannot be hid." That is to say, one's spiritual attunement cannot fall or be hidden, if it is built on the Christ Consciousness, which the high mountain represents.

Jack Finegan notes a subtle difference between the Greek form of Saying 32 (OP 1, lines 37–42) and its Coptic revision: " 'firmly established' being changed, perhaps less happily, to 'fortified.' "[1] The Greek is again to be preferred over the Coptic, in that the latter modifies the sense from "attention to the Light" to "defense against attack." This distorts Jesus' intent, as it implies an adversary, where none existed in the Saying's original form (nor in Isa. 2:2).

AFFIRMATIONS

—I am the light of the world.
—I focus on the high mountain of spiritual Truth.
—I am attuned to the infinite ideas of the Christ.
—I am strong in the Lord, and in the power of His might.

33. *Jesus said, "Preach from your housetops that which you will hear in your ear. (No. 116)*

"For no one lights a lamp and puts it under a bushel, nor does he put it in a hidden place, but rather he sets it on a lampstand so that everyone who enters and leaves will see its light." (No. 47)

The first sentence of Saying 33 (See Matt. 10:27; Luke 12:3) is followed by a scribal note, "and in the other ear." Scholars have had difficulty in deciding whether this note preserves a valid reading or adds to it. OP 1 contains only a fragment of this saying, and a different version at that. Whatever the statement's original form, the ear is a symbol of spiritual receptivity. Our text may be a way of saying: "Make active what you receive through intuition, from Divine Mind." In Mark 8:18 (See Ezek. 12:1–2), Jesus challenges his disciples: "Having eyes do you not see, and having ears do you not hear? And do you not remember?"

If the longer reading is valid, however, a further meaning is present. The statement would then also imply the difference between analysis and synthesis, between intellect and intuition. Modern psychoneurology correlates this distinction with the left and right hemispheres of the brain, respectively.

M. Marcovich, in a paper entitled "Textual Criticism of the Gospel of Thomas," makes some interesting comments:

"The point is that in primitive folklore each ear is thought of as communicating with (let us say) a separate, independent brain. The German Odin bore on his shoulders two ravens which told him, each raven in one ear, all about that was going on around: the name of the one raven was Huginn ('intellectual power'), and the name of the other Muninn ('remembrance'). The Indian magicians must blow magic into disciples' both ears; thus only will it be effective . . . . Thus the disciples of the Gnostic Jesus are expected to hear canonical sayings in one ear, and their gnostic interpretation in the other."[1]

All three Synoptic Gospels include the Parable of the Lamp (Matt. 5:15–16, Mark 4:21–22, Luke 8:16–17, 11:33). The lamp points to spiritual illumination. It symbolizes the Divine Presence, signifying life as opposed to death. The parable, also, is a challenge to show forth the qualities of God in thought, word, and deed. To those who are shy, lack confidence, or are afraid to express their talents, its message is "You *can* extend your God-given capacities into positive action."

AFFIRMATIONS

—As a child of the living God, I have both intellect and intuition. I have the Mind of Christ.

—I approach life with confidence and strength, knowing that God the Good is in charge.

—The Divine Word, the Indwelling Christ, is a lamp to my understanding and a light to my path.

—I am not afraid of people, places, or things. I am strong, confident, courageous, free. I am free with the freedom of Spirit.

---

34. *Jesus said, "If a blind man leads a blind man, they will both fall into a pit."* (No. 150)

This saying of Jesus is well attested. Matthew 15:14 also includes it: "Let them [the Pharisees] alone; they are blind guides. And if a blind man leads a blind man, both will fall into a pit." Luke 6:39 records the saying in the form of two questions: "Can a blind man lead a blind man? Will they not both fall into a pit?"

The meaning is obvious: Those who lack true understanding are not in a position to teach or guide others. They will bring trouble not only on themselves but also on those who follow them. Those of whom Jesus spoke were out of touch with the Indwelling God, and with their own psyches.

35. *Jesus said, "It is not possible for anyone to enter the house of a strong man and take it by force unless he binds his hands; then he will (be able to) ransack his house."* (No. 137)

An authentic saying of Jesus, we find parallel passages in Matthew 12:29, Mark 3:27, and Luke 11:21–22.

The strong man is not a personal devil, but a symbol of collective error. His "house" is a false belief system involving sin, disease, and lack. It seems to separate the individual from the Divine Source of his or her being. Functioning in and from the Cosmic Christ, however, Jesus had "bound the strong man" and deprived him of his seeming power. He healed the sick and the wayward, raised the dead, and restored sight to the blind. We, too, find in our own lives that truth, love, and confidence are stronger than error, hate, and fear. The "strong man" is a counterfeit from which the Mind of Christ frees us.

AFFIRMATIONS

—I give thanks for the example of Jesus the Christ in demonstrating the freeing Truth.

—I apply this Truth with the realization that God the Good is in charge.

---

36. *Jesus said, "Do not be concerned from morning until evening and from evening until morning about what you will wear."* (No. 78)

The Coptic editor greatly condensed the Greek text (OP 655, lines 1–17). This longer version is preserved in poor condition, with many letters missing. It can, however, be reconstructed as follows, drawing from Crossan, Finegan, and the text itself:

Jesus says, "Do not be concerned from morning until evening and from evening until morning, neither about your food and what you will eat, nor about your clothing and what you will wear. You are far better than the lilies which grow but do not spin. If you have one [or no] garment, what [. . . .]? Who might add to your stature? He it is who will give you your cloak."

Matthew 6:25–33, Luke 12:22–31, and the original saying in Thomas clearly draw from similar sources. These passages include sublime statements of active trust in the Divine Presence to meet our everyday needs. In the Coptic revision, however, nothing remains about trust. It only tells the reader not to be concerned "about what you will wear."

This probably means that the editor viewed the body as an obstacle to spiritual progress. From his point of view, this is the "clothing" to be rejected.

"He it is who will give you your cloak" in OP 655 refers to more than physical clothing (though that is not excluded). It expresses the archetypal image of a new garment. This means a new belief structure, grounded in conscious oneness with God. Although it exists as an internal state of true knowing, it also gives us a new image of the earth, as sustained and renewed by the Divine Presence. This includes—although it is not limited to—the body, viewed not as low and material, but as spiritual substance, light, and energy.

According to Matthew 6:33, spiritual consciousness is the key to letting go of anxious concern:

Seek first his kingdom and his righteousness [right-mindedness as well as right actions], and all these things shall be yours as well.

Both Clement of Alexandria and Origen preserve an oral tradition similar in meaning to Matthew 6:33:

Ask for the great things, and the small things shall be yours as well; and ask for the heavenly things, and the earthly things shall be yours as well.

AFFIRMATIONS

—God's prospering love blesses me, and I have plenty for every need.

—I meet life with poise and confidence, for I know that I am one with God's strength and support.

—The Mind of the Infinite shows me the needs of others, and gives me practical ideas for meeting these needs.

—I trust the universal law of increase in all my affairs, and I am abundantly prospered.

---

37. *His disciples said, "When will you become revealed to us and when shall we see you?"*
Jesus said, "When you disrobe without being ashamed and take up your garments and place them under your feet like little children and tread on them, then [will you see] the son of the living one, and you will not be afraid." (No. 378)

Similar material in John 14:22 and 16:16–19 shows that the disciples asked questions of this type. However, in comparing our two versions of Saying 37, we find that the Greek text (OP 655, lines 17–23) is much shorter:

His disciples said to him, "When will you become revealed to us and when shall we see you?"
He said, "When you disrobe and are not ashamed."

Evidently the Coptic editor took two separate sayings, and combined them in order to create a new meaning. Again he is treating garments as a metaphor for the body. To him, contempt for the body is signified by the children who stamp on their clothes.

The Greek text of Saying 37 refers to the allegory of the Garden of Eden, especially Genesis 2:25: "And the man and his wife were both naked, and were not ashamed." Nudists could use this as a proof-text. Jesus, however, taught that our Divine Father would provide us with clothing and other necessities, not that we should go about unclothed. And, he meant that it is possible to return to the state of oneness with God that the Garden of Eden symbolizes. To him, sin and guilt were not the permanent blots that later theologians believed. Rather, total forgiveness leads the way back to Eden. Also, there is only one Substance both invisible and visible, and there is nothing inherently unclean. A unitive consciousness cancels the sense of opposites, portrayed in Genesis 2:17 as "the tree of the knowledge of good and evil."

Considered separately, the second part of Saying 37 reads,

When you . . . take up your garments and place them under your feet like little children and tread on them, then [will you see] the son of the living one, and you will not be afraid.

This metaphor expresses the archetypal image of the old and new garments, and may well be genuine. The clothes trampled under our feet are various kinds of error, negation, and folly that we would do well to reject. And, as the nude children, we are ready to be clothed with new and clean garments, meaning a restored realization of the Unity of Being. When we "see the son of the living one," we are seeing ourselves as God sees us, whole, perfect, free, and thus unafraid.

Note how the Odes of Solomon compares the old and the new garments:

> And I rejected the folly cast upon the earth,
> And stripped it off and cast it from me.
> And the Lord renewed me with his garment,
> And possessed me by His light.
> And from above He gave me immortal rest,
> And I became like the land that blossoms and
>   rejoices in its fruits.
>
> (Ode 11:10–12)

The problem, then, is not the body or the earth. It is our own tendency to project false thoughts and beliefs on them. Stripped of a delusionary system, we are ready to be reclothed with the light and peace of true understanding, and prepared to receive its fruits.

AFFIRMATIONS

—I am attuned to the Unity of Being, the Good without an opposite, the Mind that is All-in-all.

—I cast off the error, negation, and folly that are foreign to my true nature.

—I receive the new garment of conscious Oneness, created after the likeness of God in true right-mindedness and wholeness.

---

38. *Jesus said, "Many times have you desired to hear these words which I am saying to you, and you have no one else to hear them from. There will be days when you will look for me and will not find me." (Nos. 290, 241)*

Jesus taught from a higher level of understanding than anyone before him. In agreement with Saying 38, Matthew 13:16–17 declares,

Blessed are your eyes, for they see, and your ears, for they hear. Truly, I say to you, many prophets and righteous men longed to see what you see, and did not see it, and to hear what you hear, and did not hear it.

"There will be days when you will look for me and will not find me." John has quite similar wordings: "You will seek me and you will not find me; where I am you cannot come" (7:34). Also, see Luke 17:22 for a related statement.

Jesus prepared his disciples, as best he could, for the time when he would no longer by physically present with them. Only after he left did they turn to the Spirit of Truth within them as their guide and support.

39. *Jesus said, "The pharisees and the scribes have taken the keys of knowledge (gnosis) and hidden them. They themselves have not entered, nor have they allowed to enter those who wish to. You, however, be as wise as serpents and as innocent as doves." (Nos. 181, 108)*

Matthew 23:13, Luke 11:52, and Thomas 39a are similar. The main difference is that in Thomas, Jesus speaks to his disciples, whereas in Matthew and Luke he denounces the scribes and Pharisees to their face. The criticism in Matthew and Luke also differs in form, though not in essential content: "You shut the kingdom of heaven against men. . . . " (Matt. 23:13); "You have taken away the key of knowledge. . . . " (Luke 11:52).

Despite the best intentions, *any* religious movement can decline and become a dry well if its members fail to keep in touch with the living Spirit. Evidently the Pharisees were initiates into the Jewish Mysteries. The "key(s) of knowledge" is a reference to these Mysteries, as is "the key of David" is Revelation 3:7. These deeper teachings, if faithfully practiced, would have led them toward the awakening to which Jesus referred. Yet according to the evidence, they neither took these teachings seriously nor shared them with the public.

Jesus, by contrast, opened his disciples to the kingdom of God within them. The Apostle Paul, in his function as a revealer of mysteries, proclaimed "the mystery hidden for ages and generations but now made manifest to his saints. To them God chose to make known how great among the Gentiles are the riches of the glory of this mystery, which is *Christ in you, the hope of glory*" (Col. 1:26–27).

"Be as wise as serpents and as innocent as doves." This is a skillful use of paradox. The serpent is an ancient symbol of wisdom; the dove, of peace and purity. Matthew 10:16 records the same simile, but places it in a different setting.

The Greek text (OP 655, lines 41–50) is extremely worn, but is sufficient to show that it contains the word *akeraios,* as does Matthew 10:16. Translated "innocent," its root meaning is "unmixed." Jesus' point is that we are not to mix our consciousness between truth and error, love and hate, faith and fear. The way to peace and safety is the unmixed realization of the Omnipresence of God.

AFFIRMATIONS

—I am open to the key of universal wisdom: Christ in us, the hope of glory.

—I am immersed in the Omnipresence, an heir to all the wisdom of the Cosmic Christ.

—I live in the unmixed consciousness of God's joy and peace.

40. *Jesus said, "A grapevine has been planted outside of the father, but being unsound, it will be pulled up by its roots and destroyed." (No. 148)*

Matthew 15:13 gives the same basic assurance: "Every plant which my heavenly Father has not planted will be rooted up." Grapevines grow wild in some parts of the Near East. Their fruit, unlike that of cultivated vines, is bitter.

All that is valid—whether in the soul, the body, or the earth—is rooted and grounded in the I AM or Cosmic Christ. The visible expression of the I AM is, symbolically, the wholesome fruit of the cultivated vine. Jesus illustrates this more fully in the Allegory of the Vine, found in John 15:1– 11.

In the inherent perfection that is God, no inharmony can be more than a temporary appearance. Only a false belief system can sustain the false vine that has been planted apart from the Father. It is destined to be pulled up by the roots and destroyed.

AFFIRMATIONS

—All thoughts, beliefs, and appearances not rooted in Divine Mind are destined to be erased.

—I abide in the true Vine, the I AM, the Cosmic Christ.

—I am that Vine, and I demonstrate its power in mind, body, and affairs.

---

41. *Jesus said, "Whoever has something in his hand will receive more, and whoever has nothing will be deprived of even the little he has." (No. 144)*

This saying of Jesus is a "floater." It appears in roughly the same form in Matthew 13:12, 25:29; Mark 4:25; and Luke 8:18, 19:26.

On the surface, these words may seem contrary to what is fair and just. In reality, they are a way of declaring that like attracts like, and that like produces like. Thus, thoughts and attitudes based on abundance and success attract and produce more abundance and success. Thoughts and attitudes based on poverty and lack attract and produce more poverty and lack.

These words of Jesus should be viewed in a positive way. People create a certain belief system for themselves, and then live within its potentials as well as its limits. Yet the Holy Spirit is always impinging on our consciousness, seeking to expand our thoughts and vision. We can, through the grace of God, change the direction of our thinking. We can sow positive thoughts and images as well as negative ones. No one need remain sick, or poor, or inadequate. The creative law is ready and willing to manifest according to the direction that we give it.

—I completely accept the fact that God's will for me is abundance.

—I trust the univeral law of increase in all my affairs, and I am abundantly prospered.

—I trust God to lead me to the place where I can best serve, and where I will be blessed in return with success and prosperity.

---

42. *Jesus said, "Become passers-by."*

The Coptic text can be taken in more than one way. William R. Schoedel translates it, "Jesus said: Come into being as you pass away."

If Jesus meant, "Become passers-by," it was a way of teaching a detached attitude, in which the individual is guided by his or her inner Self. He or she is then no longer dominated by passing appearances in the outer world.

The rendering, "Come into being as you pass away," accords well with Jesus' use of paradox. What passes away is a false belief system based on God's absence and our personal limitations. What replaces it is a growing awareness of our own status as God's unlimited Idea in an infinite universe.

Paul may have had this saying in mind when he wrote, "Though our outer nature is wasting away, our inner nature is being renewed every day" (2 Cor. 4:16).

Matthew 10:39 has somewhat the same meaning as Saying 42. If we omit the words "for my sake," we have a balanced couplet with a simple fourfold pattern:

> He who finds his life will lose it; and
> he who loses his life . . . will find it.

The phrase "for my sake" unbalances the literary structure.

Evidently the church in Antioch added it later as an endorsement of voluntary martyrdom. One would thus lose one's physical life in order to be guaranteed salvation after death. Jesus meant something quite different: someone who holds on to a negative, limited sense of life will lose out. But someone who gives up a negative self-concept and related errors will find the fullness of life as a child of God. Spiritual progress can be summed up as consciously coming into true being as old errors pass away.

—I am poised and centered in my inner Self, which is one with God.

—I am free from false, limiting beliefs and habits, through the delivering power of the Indwelling Christ.

—I am an heir of God, and a fellow heir with Jesus the Christ.

—I am free to live the healthful, joyous life of a child of the living God.

---

43. *His disciples said to him, "Who are you, that you should say these things to us?"*

Jesus said to them, "You do not realize who I am from what I say to you, but you have become like the Jews, for they either love the tree and hate its fruit or love the fruit and hate the tree."

Again we find a fourfold pattern, reflecting the Semitic literary tradition. The key phrases are also an aid to memory:

> love the tree / hate its fruit;
> love the fruit / hate the tree.

Replying to the question about his true identity, Jesus refused to give a direct answer. He knew that words alone are never the whole truth. At best, they could point to the Indwelling Christ as his disciples' true Identity as well as his own. His response treats of cause and effect. The tree is the spiritual realm of Cause, and the fruit is Its visible expression in the body and in outer action and experience. The fruit's nature is identical in essence with the nature of the tree. In other words, there is one Substance both invisible and visible.

To love the tree and hate its fruit would be to look to the spiritual Self, but to deprecate the body and eschew "material" possessions. To love the fruit and hate the tree is the opposite extreme. This would be to be interested only in the body and in worldly goods, and to reject the spiritual realm of Cause on which they are based.

Since Jesus and his disciples were themselves Jewish, the criticism of the Jews as such is out of place. The original saying must have had a more specific group or faction in mind.

The Odes of Solomon also expresses the image of the fruits of true understanding:

> For I was established and lived and was redeemed,
> And my foundations were laid on account of the Lord's hand;
> Because He has planted me.
> For He set the root,
> And watered it and endowed it and blessed it,
> And its fruits will be forever.
>
> (Ode 38:17–18)

AFFIRMATIONS

—There is a perfect Law of Expression, consisting of Creator, creative action, and creation.

—The One Creative Mind is the foundation of all existence. I am attuned to God's perfect ideas.

—The one creative action is the consciousness of the individual. My soul is a clear and unrestricted channel for the flow of Divine ideas.

—The one creation is the visible expression of this law in body, conditions, and affairs. I behold God's good flowing into outer expression through me.

—In Jesus the complete being of God is manifest; and in the Indwelling Christ I too am complete.

---

44. *Jesus said, "Whoever blasphemes against the father will be forgiven, and whoever blasphemes against the son will be forgiven, but whoever blasphemes against the holy spirit will not be forgiven either on earth or in heaven."(No. 139)*

Jesus mentions "blasphemy against the Holy Spirit" in Matthew 12:31–32, Mark 3:28–29, and Luke 12:10. He did so after the Pharisees accused him of healing by means of satanic power. No matter how ridiculous, it is possible that they meant it seriously. The parables scholar, Bernard Scott, observes, "The healing power of his [Jesus'] images was what was terrifying to his opponents, and therefore they perceived him as demonic."[1]

An important question regarding the form of Saying 44 is whether Jesus would have used a trinitarian formula. Some scholars see no reason why Jesus could not have spoken of God as Father, Son, and Holy Spirit. Others, however, note that there is no other evidence that he used such a model in his teaching program. The earlier, Greek text of this saying— assuming that is was included in the Gospel of Thomas—is lost.

In any case, it is a serious error to deny the action of the Holy Spirit in soul and body. This can only make a person sick and miserable, and that may be why Jesus used such strong language here. Yet he also taught that forgiveness is available when a person changes the direction of his or her thinking and way of life. To accept and invite the Holy Spirit's action in soul and body changes everything for the better. It is a passing from darkness into light, from spiritual blindness to intuitive sight.

AFFIRMATIONS

—I invite the action of the Holy Spirit as the one action in soul, body, and affairs.

—I accept God's healing Life and Love. I rejoice that Divine grace is at work to heal, harmonize, and adjust all that concerns me.

---

45. *Jesus said, "Grapes are not harvested from thorns, nor are figs gathered from thistles, for they do not produce fruit. A good man brings forth good from his storehouse; an evil man brings forth evil things from his evil storehouse, which is in his heart, and says evil things. For out of the abundance of the heart he brings forth evil things." (No. 90)*

This is an authentic saying of Jesus, though perhaps modified to give the negative side of cause and effect greater space. Similar material is found in Matthew 7:16–20, 12:33–35, and in Luke 6:43–45.

Jesus here teaches the mental law of cause and effect with great clarity and exactness. As within, so without. If we think and declare good, we produce good. If we think and speak evil, we produce evil. As we sow in thought and action, we reap in experience.

The seed parables are significant here. A seed is an organized potential, with the ability to fulfill itself. An acorn has a humble appearance, but in it may lie the potential to become an immense oak tree. Jesus realized that a thought, an image, or an idea is also an organized potential. Nourished by attention, feeling, and mental picturing, it will also fulfill itself.

AFFIRMATIONS

—I recognize the energy of consciousness, the dynamic factor underlying all change.

—I sow thoughts of love, wisdom, health, abundance, joy, and peace.

—I sow words that are positive, wholesome, courteous, and kind.

—I sow actions based on love, wisdom, goodwill, and good cheer.

—I relax, and let the Creative Law produce the positive effect of my sowing.

---

46. *Jesus said, "Among those born of women, from Adam until John the Baptist, there is no one so superior to John the Baptist that his eyes should be not lowered before him. Yet I have said, whichever one of you comes to be a child will be acquainted with the kingdom and will become superior to John." (No. 128)*

In the main, this saying is authentic. The mention of Adam, however, is out of place. Genesis 2:7 does not state that Adam was born of a woman, but rather that "the Lord God formed man of dust from the ground, and breathed into his nostrils the breath of life; and man became a living being."

With that exception, however, it is in accord with other references to John the Baptist. As in Matthew 11:11 and Luke 7:28, he who is least in the kingdom of heaven is greater than John. This means a difference not in degree, but in kind. Again a child represents an open and receptive state of mind. Entering the kingdom is here expressed in the true sense of *being acquainted with;* that is, in spiritual consciousness, rather than by means of physical travel.

In brief, John the Baptist typifies the left hemisphere of the brain when turned to the Superconscious Mind, or Indwelling Christ. He is the spiritualized intellect, which perceives Divine Reality as a theory or belief. He is, in symbol, *any* person who seeks to know God, and knows something about Him, but has not yet made conscious contact. John in us has a necessary function, which is *to prepare the way* for the true intuitive awareness of the Christ.

AFFIRMATIONS

—I am open and receptive to the Truth. With the spirit of a trusting child, I joyfully receive it.

—I let go of old errors. I invite the intuitive awareness of the Indwelling Christ.

---

47. *Jesus said, "It is impossible for a man to mount two horses or to stretch two bows. And it is impossible for a servant to serve two masters; otherwise, he will honor the one and treat the other contemptuously. (No. 77) No man drinks old wine and immediately desires to drink new wine. And new wine is not put into old wineskins, lest they burst; nor is old wine put into a new wineskin, lest it spoil it. An old patch is not sewn onto a new garment, because a tear would result." (Nos. 98, 216)*

These images express the absurdity of trying to think and live according to two opposing principles. Jesus taught the then current doctrine of the Two Ways, but did so with new clarity and power.

Riding a horse requires that rider and mount work together. A horse must be broken to the saddle, but the rider must respect the animal's dignity and nature. Also, novices will bounce up and down on a trotting horse. Not so experienced riders, who flow with the motion even as they are carried to their destination. We all have a belief system that carries us to a certain goal. We can, however, choose which "horse" we will ride.

Archery requires at least as much effort to master as horsemanship. To shoot an arrow well, two things are needed: (1) Muscle power, trained and developed to stretch the bow in a controlled way; and (2) total concentration in the act, but without anxiety. Both mind and muscle are likewise needed to successfully pursue the goals that we value in life.

There is, however, a deeper side to this image. The Vision of the Four Horsemen, in the Book of Revelation, includes both a white horse and an archer who rides it. The bow and arrow were a symbol of the Divine Word or Logos being spoken forth with power, in thought as well as audibly.

> And I saw, and behold, a white horse, and its rider had a bow; and a crown was given to him, and he went out conquering and to conquer. (Rev. 6:2)

The bow and arrow also appear in this symbolic sense in the Odes of Solomon:

> Walk in the knowledge of the Lord,
> And you will know the grace of the Lord generously;
> Both for His exultation and for the perfection of His knowledge.
> And His thought was like a letter,
> And His will descended from on high.
> And it was sent from a bow like an arrow
> That has been forcibly shot.
>
> (Ode 23:4-6)

The problem with having two masters (see also Matt. 6:24; Luke 16:13) is that a servant may receive contradictory orders. This can still happen in a modern corporation or agency, if an employee receives two memos from different levels of management. Trying to live according to opposing frames of reference is also difficult and perplexing. Yet it is a common human problem. Perhaps Jesus had Joshua 24:15 in mind: "Choose this day whom you will serve . . . but as for me and my house, we will serve the Lord."

The parables of the cloth and wineskins are found together not only in Thomas, but in Matthew 9:16-17, Mark 2:21-22, and Luke 5:36-39. Evidently Jesus presented both of them at the same time. In both parables, he taught the need to give up old ways of thinking and doing things, as new insights dawned and greater clarity was achieved. This included religious rites and practices, but was not limited to them. New and positive patterns of thought and action were—and still are—needed in all areas of life.

AFFIRMATIONS

—I give full attention, in thought and action, to what the Divine Spirit would have me do.

—I speak forth the Divine Word with confidence. God's works are established through His indwelling power.

—I look to God as the one all-sufficient Source of supply.

—Where needed, I let go of old beliefs, practices, and procedures. I walk in the Light as it is revealed to me.

---

48. *Jesus said, "If two make peace with each other in this one house, they will say to the mountain, 'Move away,' and it will move away." (Nos. 293, 345, 452)*

This is an authentic saying of Jesus. The Didascalia Apostolorum, a third-century Syrian work, records it in exactly the same form. Similar statements are found in Matthew 17:20, 18:19–20, 21:21–22; Mark 11:22–25; and Luke 17:5–6.

The two key images here are house and mountain. A house, in archetypal imagery, refers to one's soul or consciousness. The two who make peace within the house are not necessarily two persons. This duality can refer to the two poles of the psyche—objective and subjective, conscious and subconscious, intellect and feeling. When we bring the two into a state of harmony, energy that was formerly scattered is focused to bring order and harmony into one's life and affairs.

The mountain here is a metaphor for any obstacle that seems to retard our progress. Many people have argued over what this text means in practical terms. They agree that it refers to the power of faith, but they ask, "Does this refer to a literal mountain? Or is it a symbol only?" In my opinion, it should usually be taken as a symbol for removing obstacles that have a bearing on our everyday lives. In most cases, moving an actual mountain would be frivolous and disruptive. (It would also infringe on the right of citizens to enjoy the view!)

However, it would be dogmatic to dismiss anything good as impossible. If some situation requires moving a mountain, let us be open to the Spirit's potential for doing so through us.

AFFIRMATIONS

—I do not need to be a house divided. Through the perfect Mind of Christ, my whole psyche is brought into order, harmony, and wholeness.

—I am free from past errors and mistakes. I am attuned to the living present as I accept the Spirit's great plan for my good.

— All obstacles are removed to the Holy Spirit's invincible action in my mind, body, and affairs.

---

49. *Jesus said, "Blessed are the solitary and elect, for you will find the kingdom. For you are from it, and to it you will return."*

The solitary, translated "single ones" by William R. Schoedel, are those who find the kingdom (see Thomas 16). Again, this apparently means those who give single-minded attention to the Divine Presence. They find the kingdom as an inward experience. It is a present reality, not a mere hope for the future.

The contrast between single-minded and double-minded is important in the New Testament. For example,

The light of the body is the eye: if therefore thine eye be single, thy whole body shall be full of light. (Matt. 6:22, KJV)

For that person must not suppose that a double-minded man, unstable in all his ways, will receive anything from the Lord. (James 1:7–8)

Thomas 49 concludes, "For you are from it, and to it you will return." This applies not only to the past and future, but also to the present. That is to say, Divine Mind is not only our origin and destiny, but our present help as well. There has been an interim period of forgetting, but God is never absent. Nor can the outer appearance of things change our essential being as God's perfect Idea. We need to remember, *as a present fact,* who and what we are, even as the Prodigal Son "came to himself" (Luke 15:17). After the Last Supper, Jesus prayed,

Father, I desire that they also, whom thou hast given me, may be *with me where I am*, to behold my glory which thou hast given me in thy love for me before the foundation of the world. (John 17:24)

AFFIRMATIONS

—I am single-mindedly attentive to the Good, the True, the Beautiful.

—I am now in God's kingdom of perfect ideas. My thoughts are illumined by the Mind of Christ.

—God is fully in charge of my life, and of his universe.

—I behold, with intuitive sight, the glory that is mine before the foundation of the world.

---

50. *Jesus said, "If they say to you, 'Where did you come from?', say to them, 'We came from the light, the place where the light came into being on its own accord and established itself and became manifest through their image.' If they say to you, 'Is it you?', say, 'We are its children, and we are the elect of the living father.' If they ask you, 'What is the sign of your father in you?' say to them, 'It is movement and repose.'"*

This saying shows both Semitic imagery and the influence of Greek thought. We can't be sure how much of it Jesus actually spoke.

The imagery of light was widespread in religious writings of the first century A.D. We find this not only in Thomas, but also in the Essene writings (many of which predate the first century), the Gospel of John, Paul's letters, the Odes of Solomon, and to a lesser extent the Gospels of Matthew and Luke. In Thomas 50, the disciples' point of origin is said to be the Light, which manifests itself according to principles inherent within it.

The light and the image are linked together. Since the word for "image" is singular, this reference is not to a collection of images—nor even to individual souls—but to the Logos, the Christ Idea in the Mind of God. It is "their image" in the sense of being everyone's true Identity. The Odes of Solomon declares, in agreement,

> And there is nothing outside of the Lord,
> Because He was before anything came to be.
> And the worlds were made by His Word,
> And by the thought of His heart.
> Praise and honour to His name.
>
> (Ode 16:18–20)

"We are its [the light's] children, and we are the elect of the living father." Jesus used the metaphors of the Father and children of light. References to God as Father are numerous in the canonical gospels. "Children of light," an Essene expression, appears in Luke 16:8 and John 12:36. Also, Paul used it in 1 Thessalonians 5:5 and Ephesians 5:8. Perhaps showing the influence of Essene converts to Christianity in Damascus, Paul wrote,

> Once you were darkness, but now you are light in the Lord; walk as children of light (for the fruit of light is found in all that is good and right and true). (Eph. 5:8–9)

The sign of the Father in us "is movement and repose." Plato used this imagery in the Parmenides; it was interpreted in many ways in the centuries after him. We could say that the sign of our Father working within us is *a positive flow of ideas and images.* To the degree that we invite this healing flow, our lives move toward greater health, abundance, wisdom, and love. It is also a rest, for it is the peace of God that passes human understanding, and that keeps us attuned, in heart and mind, to the light and image of the Christ.

AFFIRMATIONS

—I am living, breathing, walking in the light of God.

—I am the image of God in expression. I show forth the glory of the kingdom.

—As the living expression of the Christ, I move into greater health, abundance, wisdom, and love.

—I rest in the peace of God that passes human understanding.

---

51. *His disciples said to him, "When will the repose of the dead come about, and when will the new world come?"*

He said to them, "What you look forward to has already come, but you do not recognize it." (No. 196)

People sometimes say at a funeral, "May God rest his (or her) soul." Tranquility is not, however, only for those who have passed on. God's peace is available now, waiting for the individual to accept it. Also, the "new world" has already come. *God is already here,* and with Him are all the resources of the Kingdom. The key is to awaken to the fact that Divine Mind is now the only Presence and the only Power, everywhere active.

The Pharisees asked Jesus the similar question of *when* the kingdom would come. He replied that *the kingdom of God is within you* (see the Introduction, Saying 3).

The error in saying that "the Lord is coming," or "the Lord will come," is the implied denial of Divine Reality in the present. The Indwelling Christ will never be more present than today. The true eschatology—to use a theological term—is to become more aware of the Divine Presence already here, and to show forth the glory and power of its truth.

AFFIRMATIONS

—God is already here. Christ is already here. The full potential of my being as God's perfect Idea is already here.

—I awaken to the Divine Presence that is forever in our midst.

—This Divine Presence shows forth Its glory and power through me.

---

52. *His disciples said to him, "Twenty-four prophets spoke in Israel, and all of them spoke in you."*

He said to them, "You have omitted the one living in your presence and have spoken only of the dead." (No. 240)

The words attributed to Jesus may be genuine. He would not have sought to downgrade the prophetic tradition, for the role of prophet is one that he himself fulfilled. Nevertheless, as the saying affirms, his main focus was on "the one living in your presence," the One Divine Reality.

The number 24 may be important, since an old Jewish book called *The Lives of the Prophets* discusses twenty-three prophets. By adding John the Baptist, the number of prophets becomes 24. Also, its most probable date of writing is A.D. 1–25.[1]

Let us assume, for the sake of argument, that the disciples' statement is also genuine, and that they had a copy of the Lives of the Prophets (then a current work) in their possession. Perhaps they wanted Jesus to review the writing, and to add comments of his own. If so, Jesus may have decided on practical grounds that their time would be better spent in other ways. It was, after all, more important to focus on the Divine Spirit that called and inspired the prophets, than on the personalities themselves.

This conclusion becomes more probable when we review the contents of the Lives of the Prophets. One of its basic traits is a monotonous narrative of the prophets' death and burial.[2] Given this rather morose literary motif, Jesus may well have replied, "You have omitted the one living in your presence and have spoken only of the dead."

53. *His disciples said to him, "Is circumcision beneficial or not?"*

He said to them, "If it were beneficial, their father would beget them already circumcised from their mother. Rather, the true circumcision in spirit has become completely profitable."

Jesus would have realized that circumcising a man or boy, in itself, makes no more sense than cutting off an ear lobe or part of a finger. If it were a good idea, a child would be born that way. It is valid to use this saying to oppose circumcision as a surgical practice.

In a Jewish context, however, circumcision has a different meaning. It is the traditional sign of the covenant between God and the Jews, especially a male's entry into this covenant relationship with God. In addition, all religious rituals have inner meanings. In the Bible, the rite in question signifies cutting off negative tendencies from the soul; for example, Deuteronomy 10:16, 30:6; Philippians 3:2–3; and Colossians 2:11. It is "the true circumcision in spirit [that] has become completely profitable."

The Odes of Solomon state:

> For the Most High circumcised me by His Holy Spirit,
> Then He uncovered my inward being towards Him,
> And filled me with His love.
>
> (Ode 11:2)

AFFIRMATIONS

—I am not bound by outer forms, rituals, and sacraments. I realize their inner meaning, which makes the outer form unnecessary.

—My baptism of water is to let the Holy Spirit cleanse, heal, and purify my soul. The false self-image of negation and death is dissolved. The realization of the living Christ in me is raised into awareness.

—My baptism of fire is to let the Holy Spirit teach me all things and fully illumine me into its Truth.

—My Lord's Supper is to awaken to my divinity, the Indwelling Christ. It is to be consciously with Jesus, and with all people, in Oneness and in Love.

—My eucharist is to realize that the whole universe is a great eucharist, the body and blood of the Cosmic Christ, filled with the Light and Substance of the All-in-all.

---

54. *Jesus said, "Blessed are the poor, for yours is the kingdom of heaven."* (No. 36)

The Gospels of Matthew and Luke include this beatitude of Jesus in a slightly different form:

Blessed are the poor in spirit, for theirs is the kingdom of heaven. (Matt. 5:3)
Blessed are you poor, for yours is the kingdom of God. (Luke 6:20)

This raises a question: Did Jesus speak of people who are poor in worldly goods? Or did he refer to those who are "poor" in some inward sense?

Jesus taught largely in the Aramaic language, among people of Aramaic culture. In that language, the word for "poor" meant not only lacking in things, but "lacking in egoistic pride." In the Peshitta text of Matthew 5:3, poor in "spirit" (*rokha*) means just that—poor in pride, humble, unassuming. Even in Luke 6:20, where he said, "blessed are *you* poor," the text states that Jesus faced his disciples—rather than the crowds, as in Matthew 5—when he gave this beatitude. This stance indicates that in Luke also, Jesus referred to an attitude of mind, not to food, clothing, and shelter, of which the common people had a meager supply.

In Jesus' sense, then, "poor" means humble and teachable. The kingdom is available to those who, regardless of station in life, are open and receptive to the Holy Spirit. This includes a willingness, as Emmet Fox wrote, "to have renounced all preconceived opinions in the whole-hearted search for God."[1] Various factors can destroy our spiritual progress, *if* we allow them to do so. These blocks include—but are not limited to—social status, pride in ancestry or rank, intellectual snobbery, and religious self-righteousness. The vessel must be made empty, so that we can receive fresh insight from the God within.

AFFIRMATIONS

—I let go of all preconceived opinions. I awaken to the inner kingdom of Christ Consciousness.

—I am open and receptive to the Holy Spirit, who teaches me all things.

---

55. *Jesus said, "Whoever does not hate his father and his mother cannot become a disciple to me. And whoever does not hate his brothers and sisters and take up his cross in my way will not be worthy of me." (Nos. 121, 122)*

This is based on an authentic saying of Jesus (parallel passage: Luke 14:26–27, see Matt. 10:37–38). The forms in Luke and Thomas, however, are dubious because they are based on mistranslations from the Aramaic. That is to say, the Aramaic word for "hate" also means "put aside." Jesus did not teach anyone to hate their family. On the contrary, he would have worked with people to help them overcome such problems. He would not want hatred for one's father, mother, brothers, or sisters to wreak havoc in anyone's personal life.

He taught us, however, to put God first with reference to our relatives. In some situations, one has to "put aside" a father, mother, brother, or sister. Even today, in many parts of Asia people give up a great deal when they change their religion. Their own families reject them and throw them out of the house as well as out of their lives. Under these conditions, converts usually become excellent and devout Christians.

We do need to count the cost of discipleship. It is said that blood is thicker than water. Yet the claims of spiritual integrity take priority over family obligations, where the two cannot be reconciled.

To "take up his cross" is not the negative and burdensome thing that is often depicted. The process does not create new emotional burdens, but dissolves existing ones. It means to erase whatever is opposed to the Allness of God. Through an inner attunement with the Indwelling Christ, we cross out sin, disease, lack, sorrow, fear, and misperceptions of every kind.

On the positive side, we have this assurance:

Jesus answered and said, Truly I say to you, There is no man who leaves houses or brothers or sisters or father or mother or wife or children or fields for my sake and for the sake of my gospel, Who shall not receive now, in this time a hundredfold, houses and brothers and sisters and maidservants and children and fields and other worldly things, and in the world to come life everlasting. (Mark 10:29–30, Lamsa translation)

AFFIRMATIONS

—I use the power of denial to cross out negative beliefs and conditions.
—I am willing to put aside all lesser loyalties. I am unified with the eternal Life, Love, and Wisdom that is God.

---

56. *Jesus said, "Whoever has come to understand the world has found (only) a corpse, and whoever has found a corpse is superior to the world." (No. 296)*

This unusual saying begins to make sense when we view it along the following lines: the covering of the human body includes a layer of dead skin, called the *epidermis.* This is outside the living skin cells known as the *derma* or *dermis.* Inside the body, and out of sight, tremendous vital processes are at work. These processes include the brain and nervous system, the circulation of the blood, the secretions of the glands, and many others. "The world"—in the sense of a false belief system—may be compared to the outer skin layer. People who believe only in what they can see, hear, smell, taste, and touch are aware only of the most external aspect of things. They know nothing of the dynamic processes of thought and belief that underlie everything that appears. They are, in this sense, aware only of what is "dead."

"Whoever has come to understand the world," then, has learned to see past surface appearances. Such people are aware of the inner dynamics of creative consciousness, and of how thoughts combined with feelings become active and manifest. Whoever has become aware of this inner reality has the key to fulfilling the Divine pattern of wholeness and well-being; he or she is "superior to the world."

AFFIRMATIONS

—I am not bound by outer appearances. I am free to release the energy of Spirit through my consciousness.

—As I attune myself to the Christ within, the inner kingdom is made visible.

---

57. *Jesus said, "The kingdom of the father is like a man who had [good] seed. His enemy came by night and sowed weeds among the good seed. The man did not allow them to pull up the weeds; he said to them, 'I am afraid that you will go intending to pull up the weeds and pull up the wheat along with them.' For on the day of the harvest the weeds will be plainly visible, and they will be pulled up and burned." (No. 2)*

The seed parables of Jesus represent the sowing of ideas in the mind. They equate thoughts and seeds in the sense that both are organized potentials, with the ability to fulfill themselves. Each seed parable, in addition, makes at least one point unique to itself. In the Wheat and the Tares (found in a longer form in Matt. 13:24–30), we find that both positive thoughts (good seed) and negative ones (weed seed) produce results after their kind. Also—and here is a key point in both versions—the difference is not always readily apparent until one has gained a certain level of spiritual maturity. (Evidently the weeds in the parable are darnel, a form of grass that resembles wheat in its earlier stages of growth.) The weeds in the story are thus allowed to grow for a time with the wheat, until "the day of the harvest." Then the separation is made.

Unlike the Gospel of Matthew, Thomas includes no interpretation for this parable, because it was not in the sources that the compiler of Thomas used. Although the parable itself is certainly genuine, the comments found in Matthew 13:37–43 are a distortion of Jesus' meaning. They are a product of the later Church, and reflect an attempt to reinterpret his words in light of later conditions.

AFFIRMATIONS

—I have a growing sense of the difference between true and false, positive and negative, real and unreal.

—I seek Divine guidance and right action in this situation. I know what to do, and how to do it.

—I focus on what is true, positive, and real as it is revealed to me.

---

58. *Jesus said, "Blessed is the man who has suffered and found life."*

Passages with a similar meaning appear both in the Bible and in extracanonical sources. Sayings 68 and 69 in Thomas, and Barnabas 7:11 (see No. 320 in Crossan's workbook), also mention suffering as a stepping-stone toward spiritual wholeness. Biblical passages include the following:

Come to me, all who labor and are heavy laden, and I will give you rest. (Matt. 11:28)
Blessed are those who are persecuted for righteousness' sake, for theirs is the kingdom of heaven. (Matt. 5:10)

Sayings of this kind do not refer primarily to persecution by other people. They point to the need to get rid of emotional garbage, in order to find true life and the peace of God. There is certain to be inner anguish as old and false beliefs resist the growing awareness of Divine Reality. However, there is an end to such suffering. Also, when the cleansing process is largely completed, the rewards are great. This is expressed in various ways: as finding life (Thomas 58), knowing the Father (Thomas 69), attaining the kingdom (Barnabas), and having the kingdom of heaven and receiving rest (Matthew).

AFFIRMATIONS

—Even when God appears to be absent, His presence guides and sustains me.

—Even when there appears to be darkness, I am surrounded and enfolded in God's Light and Love.

---

59. *Jesus said, "Take heed of the living one while you are alive, lest you die and seek to see him and be unable to do so."*

This saying can be variously interpreted. "The living one" could refer to

1. God as Divine Presence, the giver and sustainer of life
2. Jesus, with reference to his resurrection
3. The Indwelling Christ, the eternal Self of everyone.

"Lest you die" also can be taken in more than one way. It could refer to bodily death or to dying spiritually.

Jesus emphasized the need to contact Divine Reality now, rather than at some future time. Because humanity has largely forgotten its true Source in Spirit, knowing God is not automatic—either on this plane or on "the other side." We need to turn to the Light wherever we are. Then we will be able to receive the fullness of life that God has prepared for us.

In the omnipresence of God, the only place is here, and the only time is now. More than enough has been said about what God did in the past, and will do in the future. Reviewing God's action in the past is valuable only to the extent that it illuminates what is potential in the present. As Paul declared,

It is no longer I who live, but Christ who lives in me; and the life I *now* live in the flesh I live by faith in the Son of God. (Gal. 2:20)

AFFIRMATIONS

—I reject the myth of time. Right now, just as I am, I turn to the Light of God.

—I live in eternity now. I am one with the Indwelling Christ now, and I awaken to this truth.

---

60. *They saw a Samaritan carrying a lamb on his way to Judea. He said to his disciples, "That man is round about the lamb."*

They said to him, "So that he may kill it and eat it."

He said to them, "While it is alive, he will not eat it, but only when he has killed it and it has become a corpse."

They said to him, "He cannot do so otherwise."

He said to them, "You, too, look for a place for yourselves within repose, lest you become a corpse and be eaten."

The central figure of this dialogue is a Samaritan who is about to butcher a lamb and eat it. Therefore, the symbology of *the Samaritan* and of *the lamb* need to be considered.

The Samaritans were a mixed race of both Assyrian and Hebrew ancestry. As such, they typify a mixed state of consciousness based on duality and conflict. Similarly, Charles Fillmore wrote that "The Samaritans signify mixed thoughts, partly worldly and partly religious."[1]

The lamb, in contrast, represents innocence in the sense of an unmixed or undivided consciousness, centered in the Unity of Being. In Jesus' simile, the Samaritan is preparing to kill the lamb. This is a warning not to let the "Samaritan" destroy the "lamb" within our own psyches. We are called to find the place of rest, of God-realization within us. Failing to do so, we would become a "sacrificial lamb" and be eaten by the Samaritan.

—There is only one Presence and one Power in my life, God the Good, All-governing.

—I find the center of inner peace within me. I rest in the omnipresence of God.

—I am conscious of the infinite nature of God as Love, Life, Truth, Mind, and Substance. I show forth this Divine nature in positive and harmonious ways.

---

61. *Jesus said, "Two will rest on a bed: the one will die, and the other will live."* (No. 204)

Salome said, "Who are you, man, that you . . . have come up on my couch and eaten from my table?"

Jesus said to her, "I am he who exists from the undivided. I was given some of the things of my father." (No. 133)

. . . "I am your disciple."

. . . "Therefore I say, if he is destroyed, he will be filled with light, but if he is divided, he will be filled with darkness." (No. 76)

This dialogue is not an actual record of Jesus visiting a woman named Salome. It is a literary device, invented to frame some of Jesus' sayings. The name Salome, in its noun form, means "peace, well-being"; and as an adjective, "whole, complete, perfect." She appeared often, *as a symbol,* in religious writings of the second and third centuries; for example, the Gospel According to the Egyptians, the Birth of Mary, the Apocalypse of James, and the Pistis Sophia.

"Two will rest on a bed: the one will die, the other will live." Luke 17:34 records a similar statement: "I tell you, in that night there will be two in one bed; one will be taken and the other left." Because the original setting of this statement is uncertain, its precise meaning is also unclear. Both Luke and Thomas propose an unlikely context.

"I am he who exists from the undivided." Coptic scholars find this passage difficult to translate, but it was probably authentic in its original form. It resembles Jesus' I AM statements as found largely in the Gospel of John. What we have is a prayer of identification, in which Jesus identifies himself with the I AM or Indwelling Christ. This is our true Identity—as well as that of Jesus—which inheres in the undivided nature of the One Mind.

"I was given some of the things of my father." The word "some" is restrictive, when compared with Jesus' statement in Matthew 11:27 and Luke 10:22: "All things have been delivered to me by my Father." In addition, John 3:35 declares, "The Father loves the Son, and has given all things into his hand." Not all Coptic scholars, however, include "some" in their translation of Thomas 61. Jesse J. Sell translates, "To me was given from the things of My Father." Similarly, William R. Schoedel renders the passage: "I was given the things of my Father."

According to worldly logic, if Jesus has received everything from the Father there is nothing left for the rest of us. Jesus, however, did not refer here to "physical" things, but to the divine ideas that underlie all substance, regardless of its form. Jesus' full access to the Father states our own position with reference to God, rather than excluding it. It is said that if we give an apple to another, that other person then has it and we don't. If we give an idea, however, both continue to share it without limitation. Divine ideas are like that, and more—they are infinite, eternal, and inexhaustible.

"Therefore I say, if he is destroyed, he will be filled with light, but if he is divided, he will be filled with darkness." This couplet follows the Semitic literary form, and is probably based on an authentic saying of Jesus. According to the Coptic Gnostic Library Project, its key terms are translated as follows:

> destroyed / filled with light
> divided / filled with darkness

Given the difficulties at this point in the text, however, the translation "destroyed" remains open to question. Edgar Hennecke translates "equal"; William R. Schoedel shows "deserted"; and the 1977 edition of *The Nag Hammadi Library* uses "undivided." As "undivided" is obviously the antonym of "divided" in the second line, it makes sense from the standpoint of literary balance.

Also, if we retain the word "undivided," the saying affirms the principle of the "single eye" mentioned in Matthew 6:22-23 and Luke 11:34–36 (see James 1:5–8). It contrasts two ways of viewing things: (1) within the unity of all life in the One Mind, or (2) according to the illusion of opposing forces. A unified consciousness is equated with light, and the Light of God expresses itself through such unity. A divided mind leads to confusion and perceptual darkness.

AFFIRMATIONS

—I live, move, and have my being in the undivided nature of Infinite Mind.

—All that the Father has is mine to use, to enjoy, to share, and to circulate.

—I rejoice in the undivided nature of all Being. I am filled with the Light of the Christ in mind, body, and affairs.

---

62. *Jesus said, "It is to those [who are worthy of my] mysteries that I tell my mysteries. Do not let your left hand know what your right hand is doing." (Nos. 67, 143)*

Because of a gap in the manuscript, the precise meaning of this statement about the mysteries is an educated guess. The mysteries were secret societies who had their own spiritual teachings and private rituals. To a degree, Jesus followed this ancient pattern. He offered both an exoteric teaching for the general public, and an esoteric teaching for an inner circle. Jesus' motive, however, was not secrecy *per se*. When a person made a firm commitment to become a disciple, no teaching was withheld.

Mark 4:11 states, "To you has been given the secret [in Greek, *mustērion*] of the kingdom of God, but for those outside everything is in parables" (see also Matt. 13:11, Luke 8:10). The Odes of Solomon also mention the mysteries:

> Keep my mystery, you who are kept by it;
> Keep my faith, you are who kept by it.
> (Ode 8:10)

The statement "Do not let your left hand know what your right hand is doing" also appears in the Gospel of Matthew. There, however, it is related to giving charity without seeking a reward:

Thus, when you give alms, sound no trumpet before you, as the hypocrites do in the synagogues and in the streets, that they may be praised by men. Truly, I say to you, they have their reward. But when you give alms, do not let your left hand know what your right hand is doing, so that your alms may be in secret; and your Father who sees in secret will reward you. (Matt. 6:2–4)

In a broader sense, the left / right hand image refers to the difference between intuition (left hand, right brain hemisphere) and intellect (right hand, left brain hemisphere). In essence, we are told not to let the calculating intellect prevent those actions that our intuition guides us to do. Nor are we to do the things that our intellect favors, if our intuition rejects them. This is not an excuse to avoid thinking. The saying does imply, however, that we have access to a far greater range of awareness than is possible through logic and analysis alone.

AFFIRMATIONS

—I am in the Presence of God, the One Creative Mind, who gives me a new sense of direction. I know what to do and how to proceed.

—The guiding light of the Holy Spirit shines before me and makes plain my way.

---

63. *Jesus said, "There was a rich man who had much money. He said, 'I shall put my money to use so that I may sow, reap, plant, and fill my storehouse with produce, with the result that I shall lack nothing.' Such were his intentions, but that same night he died. Let him who has ears hear." (Nos. 18, 130)*

This is a shorter version of the Parable of the Rich Fool, also found in Luke 12:16–20. Although the two differ in detail, they share a common ground: the human individual is not self-sufficient. The rich man in the parable made careful, logical (we might say today, "left hemispheric") plans for future pleasure, abundance, and security. Yet his intentions failed when he abruptly died.

In brief, then, the parable's sole character put wealth before wisdom and ended up with neither. The Book of Proverbs expresses a sounder attitude. It affirms that God is the Source of both wealth and wisdom:

> Happy is the man who finds wisdom,
> and the man who gets understanding,
> for the gain from it is better than gain from silver
> and its profit better than gold.
> She is more precious than jewels,
> and nothing you desire can compare with her.
> Long life is in her right hand;
> in her left hand are riches and honor.
> Her ways are ways of pleasantness,
> and all her paths are peace.
>
> (Prov. 3:13–17)

Also, the prophet Jeremiah declared (9:23–24),

Thus says the Lord: "Let not the wise man glory in his wisdom, let not the mighty man glory in his might, let not the rich man glory in his riches; but let him who glories glory in this, that he understands and knows me, that I am the Lord who practices steadfast love, justice, and righteousness in the earth; for in these things I delight, says the Lord."

AFFIRMATIONS

—I rejoice in the intuitive wisdom that the Christ Spirit gives me.

—I am open and receptive to Divine understanding.

—Both riches and honor are mine, from the Divine Presence in whom I live and have my being.

---

64. *Jesus said, "A man had received visitors. And when he had prepared the dinner, he sent his servant to invite the guests. He went to the first one and said to him, 'My master invites you.' He said, 'I have claims against some merchants. They are coming to me this evening. I must go and give them my orders. I ask to be excused from the dinner.' He went to another and said to him, 'My master has invited you.' He said to him, 'I have just bought a house and am required for the day. I shall not have any spare time.' He went to another and said to him, 'My master invites you.' He said to him, 'My friend is going to get married, and I am to prepare the banquet. I shall not be able to come. I ask to be excused from the dinner.' He went to another and said to him, 'My master invites you.' He said to* him, 'I have just bought a farm, and I am on my way to collect the rent. I shall not be able to come. I ask to be excused.' The servant returned and said to his master, 'Those whom you invited to the dinner have asked to be excused.' The master said to his servant, 'Go outside to the streets and bring back those whom you happen to meet, so that they may dine.' Businessmen and merchants will not enter the places of my father." (No. 12)

Jesus gave this parable at least twice, in different versions. The texts in Matthew and Luke and in Thomas differ in such a manner than they cannot be based on a single source. Although I will not give a detailed literary analysis here, I will say that the parable in Thomas is more authentic than the versions in Matthew 22:1–14 and Luke 14:16–24. Only the doubtful statement at the end—regarding the businessmen and merchants—appears to be secondary. In the Lucan version, 14:21b–22 and 14:24 are later additions. The parallel in Matthew is even more corrupt, in that 22:1–14 includes what were originally *three* separate parables, in whole or in part.

This parable can be validly interpreted on at least two levels: first, Jesus is saying that life is more like a banquet than a vale of tears. The kingdom of God is indeed like a banquet. A feast of divine ideas is laid out before our intuition, and all are invited to partake. In fact, as the story implies, God *seeks us out* so that we may more readily return to conscious harmony with him. Yet many, being preoccupied with worldly concerns, make a variety of excuses for not attending. They choose to rely solely on their own efforts to achieve success and happiness. They are the losers—and yet the opportunity is there.

Second, the host can be taken to refer not to God, but to ourselves. In this sense, the remarkable thing is that the host's normal expectations in life are shattered. Everyone on his guest list refuses to attend. This is like the person who has viewed life in a strictly material sense, and has failed to understand the laws of mind and Spirit. His or her belief system, being false, suddenly and unexpectedly collapses. It no longer works. Life will again become workable, however, if he or she gains a new and truer frame of reference based on the omnipresence of God and the formative power of thought.

AFFIRMATIONS

—I accept the Father's invitation to his feast. I feast on divine ideas, intuitions, and insights.

—I give thanks that in the kingdom of God, life is not a vale of tears. It is a banquet. It is a joy to be alive, to be one with God, and to see the good in everything.

—I am willing to see things differently. I am open and receptive to the Truth, and I receive it joyously.

65. *He said, "There was a good man who owned a vineyard. He leased it to tenant farmers so that they might work it and he might collect the produce from them. He sent his servant so that the tenants might give him the produce of the vineyard. They seized his servant and beat him, all but killing him. The servant went back and told his master. The master said, 'Perhaps he did not recognize them.' He sent another servant. The tenants beat this one as well. Then the owner sent his son and said, 'Perhaps they will show respect to my son.' Because the tenants knew that it was he who was the heir to the vineyard, they seized him and killed him. Let him who has ears hear."* (Nos. 11, 130)

66. *Jesus said, "Show me the stone which the builders have rejected. That one is the cornerstone."* (No. 173)

Of the four existing versions of this parable, that in Thomas is closest to its original form.[1] Also, all four have the Simile of the Rejected Cornerstone following directly after. Since Thomas, in a literary sense, is independent of Matthew, Mark, and Luke, it is certain that Jesus himself connected the two:

SOURCE DOCUMENT	WICKED HUSBANDMEN	REJECTED CORNERSTONE
OT Book of Psalms	———	118:22–23
Matthew	21:33–41	21:42
Mark	12:1–9	12:10–11
Luke	20:9–16	20:17
Thomas	Saying 65	Saying 66

The early Church tended to interpret the vineyard as a metaphor for Israel, as in Isaiah 5:1–7. In Jesus' own symbology, however, the vineyard represents the cultivated area of the mind. The tenant farmers are false beliefs and attitudes that have usurped the authority of the Indwelling Christ in the soul. The Indwelling Christ is the son in the parable, the true "heir to the vineyard." The usurpers act rashly and wickedly, until they are thrown out of the vineyard and destroyed.

Having given the parable, Jesus shifted his metaphors to those of Psalms 118:22. In the building trade, a cornerstone's measurements had to be exact, because they determined all the dimensions of a house. The cornerstone, as a symbol of the Allness/Omnipresence of God, gives the correct basis for thinking. This truth, and it alone, provides a sound frame of reference for building one's house (soul or consciousness) along correct lines. The stone that the builders rejected is to become the head of the corner.

—I invite the Indwelling Christ to take complete charge of my soul.

—I reject what is false, demeaning, and limiting. I affirm my divine inheritance as a son (daughter) of God, and as a fellow heir with Jesus the Christ.

—I accept the omnipresence of God as the true foundation of all thought. Through the One healing, harmonizing, prospering Presence, all my needs are met.

---

67. _Jesus said, "If one who knows the all still feels a personal deficiency, he is completely deficient."_

It is possible that this statement continues the original context of Sayings 65–66. For its reference to the All agrees with the symbology of the Cornerstone, which in turn follows Jesus' Parable of the Wicked Husbandmen. The parable, using the image of the son and heir of the vineyard, really points to our own Divine Self which is one with the All.

In any case, the point of Saying 67 is well taken. One can praise God to the heights, but in such a way that one's own individuality is denied. The one who knows the All, but fails to know his or her true Identity, remains in a consciousness of lack. This is a key issue in Jesus' teaching: _To affirm and demonstrate the oneness of God the Divine Source, and humankind as God's perfect Idea, the Christ._ God's Omnipresence is affirmed in a way that cleanses, heals, inspires, and empowers us on an individual level.

It is essential, then, that we do not view the Allness of God as opposed to our own individuality. We are eternally within that Unity of Being, one with Jesus and heirs to the whole estate. We are not servants, robots, or machines. As Jesus declared after the Last Supper:

No longer do I call you servants [by definition, inferior], for the servant does not know what his master is doing; but I have called you friends [by definition, equal], for all that I have heard from my Father I have made known to you. (John 15:15)

—I am conscious of the Divine Presence at all times. All my needs are met in Divine Order, according to God's unchanging laws.

—The Allness of God is my all-sufficiency in all things.

—I find my Identity in the All's perfect Idea, the Christ.

---

68. _Jesus said, "Blessed are you when you are hated and persecuted. Wherever you have been persecuted they will find no place."_

69. *Jesus said, "Blessed are they who have been persecuted within themselves. It is they who have truly come to know the father. Blessed are the hungry, for the belly of him who desires will be filled." (Nos. 39, 43)*

The Gospel of Thomas points primarily to the *inner* sense of persecution (see Thomas 58; Matt. 5:10–12; Luke 6:22-23). The problem is in our own belief system, not in other people. In this respect, Thomas 69 is most explicit. It is good that the false clashes with the true in the soul, as long as the individual holds steadfastly to the Unity of Being. It is at such times of inner struggle that the greatest spiritual growth takes place, and that negative conditioning of the past is overcome. The end result is that we "have truly come to know the father." In this sense, a time of persecution can be a time of joy.

"Wherever you have been persecuted they will find no place" (68b). When the inner healing is complete, nothing remains within the psyche that is contrary to the Indwelling Christ. All is cleansed, renewed, and transformed. And, in the same process, the body is also made whole.

"Blessed are the hungry, for the belly of him who desires will be filled." The canonical gospels give two other versions of this beatitude:

Blessed are those who hunger and thirst for righteousness [right-mindedness], for they shall be satisfied. (Matt. 5:6)

Blessed are you that hunger now, for you shall be satisfied. (Luke 6:21)

The wording in Matthew refers to satisfying spiritual needs, and that in Thomas to the need for food. Luke's version does not specify whether the hunger is spiritual or physical. We should not, however, give undue weight to these variant readings. The Divine Presence meets human needs on all levels. Also, statements in the Bible and related literature can often—as here—be validly taken either as concepts or as metaphors. Words that appear "literal" to the left brain hemisphere are often figurative. Even in Thomas 69b, then, the need for bodily nourishment can represent the need to be nourished by the living Spirit within us, and to assimilate Divine ideas.

AFFIRMATIONS

—I hold to the Truth that there is only one Presence and one Power in my life, God the Good, All-governing.

—The prospering power of God is at work in my affairs, and I am abundantly supplied. All the needs of soul, mind, and body are met.

---

70. *Jesus said, "That which you have will save you if you bring it forth from yourselves. That which you do not have within you will kill you if you do not have it within you."*

This saying of Jesus points to the inner dynamics that make all the difference in our everyday lives. The words may be somewhat garbled in transmission, but their intent is still clear. The power of the Christ within, if brought to conscious awareness, will establish wholeness in mind, body, and outer experiences. If it is bottled up or repressed, however, destructive emotional patterns will continue to function on a subliminal level. As a result, our psychic energy will be inverted to wreak destruction in all areas of life.

Jesus' whole pastoral ministry, including his healings, became workable through release of the spiritual power that indwells all. We need to emphasize that this Truth was not only in him, but equally in his disciples and clients, *and in us today.* Effective counseling is still based on the capacity of the God within—whatever we choose to call it—to heal and transform consciousness.

AFFIRMATIONS

—The same Power that raised Jesus from the dead is now at work in me, and in all people.

—This inner Principle, whose essence is Love, now brings forth healing, harmony, and deliverance in my soul (mind) (body) (affairs).

—I now accept, release, and manifest the indwelling energy of Spirit.

---

71. *Jesus said, "I shall [destroy this] house, and no one will be able to build it."* (No. 211)

Although this is well documented as a saying of Jesus, the question of *context* needs to be considered. Of course, he could have used it more than once and in different forms. According to John 2:19, "Jesus answered them 'Destroy this temple, and in three days I will raise it up.' " John 2:21 continues, "he spoke of the temple of his body." In the Gospel of John, then, he uses this saying to predict his own resurrection.

Jesus' opponents claimed that he had referred to the temple in Jerusalem. This, however, is as far-fetched as it was slanderous (see Matt. 22:60–61; 27:39–40; Mark 14:57–58; 15:29; Acts 6:14). It would have served no purpose to dare someone to tear down Herod's temple—an enormous edifice—and then to offer to rebuild it in three days.

The variant in Thomas, however, refers neither to his body nor to the temple. It mentions not a *temple,* but a *house.* In this form, the saying teaches that the Indwelling Christ has the capacity to destroy whatever "house," or false belief system, exists within the individual and in society. Also, once we have awakened to the reality of the God within, no one will be able to restore the web of error and illusion that once prevailed.

AFFIRMATIONS

—The Indwelling Christ is the eternal Source and Pattern of health, wisdom, love, harmony, abundance, joy, and peace.

—This inner Truth, which I AM, dissolves all that is false within me. I claim my full divine inheritance now.

---

72. *A man said to him, "Tell my brothers to divide my father's possessions with me."*

He said to him, "O man, who has made me a divider?"

He turned to his disciples and said to them, "I am not a divider, am I?" (No. 482)

The same incident appears in Luke 12:13–14. The Gospel of Luke links it to the Parable of the Rich Fool (12:16–20), with 12:15 serving as a transition. Thomas, however, lists the parable separately (Saying 63). Therefore, the linkage in Luke is probably a literary device used to connect two originally separate events.

The Lucan parallel reads,

One of the multitude said to him, "Teacher, bid my brother divide the inheritance with me." But he said to him, "Man, who made me a judge or divider over you?"

Thomas records Jesus' reply in more general terms: "Who has made me a divider?" It also includes an aside to the disciples: "I am not a divider, am I?" In the literal sense, Jesus was neither a judge nor a scribe of the type who were called on to settle such cases. Hence it was not his function to adjudicate claims of this kind. In a larger sense, he meant that *Oneness, not division or confrontation, is the nature of God's universe.* The Christ or Inheritance, which Jesus represents, comes into our consciousness not to create false divisions, but to unify us with God and with each other. Oneness is already true, but we need to be awakened to its reality and power.

AFFIRMATIONS

—The Infinite Mind of Christ is now at work in myself and in everyone.

—I see God's universe as whole, complete, and perfect, ready and able to supply every human need.

—I affirm that my own needs are now met, in accordance with Divine Order and right action. I rejoice that this is so.

---

73. *Jesus said, "The harvest is great but the laborers are few. Beseech the lord, therefore, to send out laborers to the harvest." (No. 99)*

Sayings 73, 74, and 75 have a common theme: the contrast between the many and the few.

Matthew 9:37 and Luke 10:2 also record Saying 73. "The harvest is great but the laborers are few" was a folk saying that Jesus applied in a new way. As he sent out his disciples to minister in Galilee, he noted how many people needed their help. Yet so few were ready and equipped to serve.

The account in Matthew summarizes the threefold nature of Christian ministry:

And Jesus went about all the cities and villages, *teaching* in their synagogues and *preaching* the gospel of the kingdom, and *healing* every disease and every infirmity. When he saw the crowds, he had compassion for them, because they were harassed and helpless, like sheep without a shepherd. (Matt. 9:35–36)

AFFIRMATIONS

—I am ready and willing to do the work that God would have me do, whatever that work may be.

—The inner potential to do this work is already mine. Through the indwelling Spirit of God, this potential is released in and through me.

---

74. *He said, "O lord, there are many around the drinking trough, but there is nothing in the cistern."*

Coptic scholars differ as to how this saying should be translated. The translation of Thomas O. Lambdin, shown here, is plausible in that it agrees with the prophetic tradition. Jeremiah 2:13 declares,

> My people have committed two evils:
> they have forsaken me,
> the fountain of living waters,
> and hewed out cisterns for themselves,
> broken cisterns, that can hold no water.

The many are those who try to drink spiritually from an empty trough, supplied by a broken cistern. That is to say, the many are willing to accept someone else's opinions about spiritual Truth, without examining those beliefs for themselves. They seek God in the broken cisterns of creeds, rituals, and outer forms. The few are different. They seek first-hand contact with God, "the fountain of living waters." They fulfill the prophecy in Jeremiah 31:33 by discovering the inner Law, and finding it written on their hearts.

AFFIRMATIONS

—I live in the immediate Presence of the Infinite. I now receive the fountain of living waters, and I am whole.

—I have peace like a river in my soul.

---

75. *Jesus said, "Many are standing at the door, but it is the solitary who will enter the bridal chamber." (No. 302)*

As with Sayings 16 and 49, we are opting for William R. Schoedel's translation: read "single ones" instead of "solitary." Again, in keeping with Matthew 6:22, to be "single" means to be totally attuned to the Divine Omnipresence.

A related saying (50b) in the Dialogue of the Savior, also found at Nag Hammadi, declares, "When you rid yourselves of jealousy, then you will clothe yourselves in light and enter the bridal chamber."

Within the meaning of these sayings, ridding oneself of jealousy has an obvious connection with becoming single. Jealousy requires the belief that some good, possessed by another, is inaccessible to us. Realizing the Unity of Being, however, eliminates this belief because we discover that nothing good is withheld from us. We are then no longer attracted to unwholesome conditions of dependency on others, for we find that we—as well as all other people—can tap the Divine Source directly to meet every need.

Used as a metaphor, the term "bride of Christ" is a valid expression. The soul (the bride) is to unite inwardly with the Indwelling Christ (the groom). This unity is the symbolic bridal chamber. In consummating this union, the Christ impregnates the soul with divine ideas. From this joining of Spirit and soul, everything good, wholesome, and positive issues forth into everyday life.

AFFIRMATIONS

—I identify with the Indwelling Christ as my true Self.
—As I give total attention to the Divine Presence, I am healed, harmonized, and renewed in soul and body.

---

76. *Jesus said, "The kingdom of the Father is like a merchant who had a consignment of merchandise and who discovered a pearl. That merchant was shrewd. He sold the merchandise and bought the pearl alone for himself. You too, seek his unfailing and enduring treasure where no moth comes near to devour and no worm destroys." (Nos. 6, 74)*

The Synoptic Gospels include roughly the same material, but arrange it differently. The Parable of the Pearl also appears in Matthew 13:45–46. A variant Parable of the Hidden Treasure is in Thomas as Saying 109, but the biblical version is found with the Pearl—as a twin parable—in Matthew 13:44. Thomas 76, however, adds the admonition to "seek his unfailing and enduring treasure." This admonition resembles statements found in Matthew 6:20 and Luke 12:33. Matthew 6:19–21 reads,

Do not lay up for yourselves treasures on earth, where moth and rust consume and where thieves break in and steal, but lay up for yourselves treasures in heaven, where neither moth nor rust consumes and where thieves do not break in and steal. For where your treasure is, there will your heart be also.

The Pearl of Jesus' parable is the greatest of all treasures. It symbolizes the Indwelling Christ, our true Identity in Divine Mind. The parable also gives three basic steps in claiming this treasure. The first is to *discover* Its reality. The second is to *sell*, or give up, all contrary beliefs and opinions. The third is to *buy* it; that is, to receive and become conscious of this Truth for ourselves. This does not mean a mere passive acceptance. It requires an effort at total attunement to the Allness/ Omnipresence of God.

The *moth,* the *rust* (or *worm,* depending how one considers the underlying Greek), and the *thief* suggest the practical hazards of a worldly state of mind. When we place our security in outer things and conditions, we are—to use a modern metaphor—skating on thin ice. When we base our security on the Divine Presence, however, we receive God's perfect ideas and are inwardly transformed. This is what Jesus meant by laying up treasures in heaven. When we do so, we are both self-reliant in the highest sense, and within the orbit of God's protection and supply. We then fear no evil, for we have a vital connection with the living God.

AFFIRMATIONS

—I discover the Indwelling Christ as the greatest of all treasures.
—I let go of all beliefs and opinions the reject its reality.
—I joyfully receive the Indwelling Christ as my true Identity.
—As I commune with the Divine Presence, I receive God's perfect ideas. I am transformed by the renewal of my mind.

---

77. *Jesus said, "It is I who am the light which is above them all. It is I who am the all. From me did the all come forth, and unto me did the all extend.*

Split a piece of wood, and I am there. Lift up the stone, and you will find me there." (No. 304)

Of the five sentences in this saying, only the first three really belong here. OP 1, one of the earlier Greek fragments of the Gospel of Thomas, links the wood and the stone with Saying 30.

The three sentences are prayers of identification. They declare that I AM (the Logos or Christ) is the Light that is above all, and in all, and has dominion over all. These statements sound extravagant, but they resemble those that Jesus used in the Gospel of John. Obviously, he did not thus refer to himself on a human level. Jesus, as a person, was obviously *not* all; this statement is meaningless to the physical senses. Christ on a cosmic level, however, *is* all, being the Father's total Idea of Himself.

In the Gospel of John, Jesus declared, "I AM the light of the world" (8:12, 9:5). Matthew 5:14 extends this identification to others: "*You* are the light of the world." Again, the Prologue of John states, "All things were made through him" (1:3), and "The true light that enlightens every man was coming into the world" (1:9).

According to Paul, quoting a very early hymn in Colossians 1:15–20: "He [the *eikōn* or Cosmic Christ] is before all things, and in him all things hold together" (1:17). "For in him all the fulness of God was pleased to dwell" (1:19). Ephesians 1:23 affirms "the fulness of him who fills all in all." From the same universal point of view, we read, "Here there cannot be Greek and Jew, circumcised and uncircumcised, barbarian, Scythian, slave, free man, but Christ is all, and in all" (Col. 3:11).

In the apocryphal Acts of Peter, we read,

Thou art perceived of the spirit only, thou art unto me father, thou my mother, thou my brother, thou my friend, thou my bondsman, thou my steward: thou art the All and the All is in thee: and thou Art, and there is nought else that IS save thee only. (from Chapter 39, translated by M. R. James)[1]

The Gospel of Truth also contains relevant statements; for example,

For he discovered them in himself, and they discovered him in themselves, the incomprehensible, inconceivable one, the Father, the perfect one, the one who made the all, while the all is within him and the all has need of him. (lines 18:29–35, translated by George W. MacRae)[2]

Jesus did not invent the I AM statement. He did, however, lift its use out of superstition and magic, and placed it on a basis of the Unity of Being. Others had used this method to identify themselves with what they conceived to be a lesser god, or goddess, or angel, or demon. In so doing, they sought to be empowered in specific ways. Jesus, by identifying himself with the All-in-all and not with any limited factor, was able to demonstrate his mastery of the whole estate, even resurrection from the dead.

The references to the stone and wood have been criticized because they seem to make Jesus a pantheist. Pantheism in the correct sense, however, includes a belief that God is somehow trapped in created things. Taken in context with Matthew 18:18–20 and Saying 30, the two references fail to support this view. In fact, they yield the reverse meaning: God's power is unlimited *because* He indwells all, including wood and stone. Or more precisely, *wood, stone, and all things indwell God.*

Jesus meant, in essence, that Omnipresence permeates and includes all things, but is never limited by any form. The I AM, the Cosmic Christ, is under the stone and within the wood. Even the humble worms and insects that one can find in such places—and that Jesus, being in close rapport with the earth, would have observed—are alive with God's Life, for God is the Principle of all life. He also said (Luke 12:6–7, see also Matt. 10:29–31),

Are not five sparrows sold for two pennies? And not one of them is forgotten before God. Why, even the hairs of your head are all numbered. Fear not; you are of more value than many sparrows.

AFFIRMATIONS

—I cease forever to call myself sick, sinful, poor, inadequate, or unhappy. These are false identifications that have nothing to do with me.

—I AM the light of the world. I AM all that God is, in active expression. The All-in-all expresses Itself through me as good health, personal integrity, abundant supply, confidence, and joy.

—I cease forever to call others sick, sinful, poor, inadequate, or unhappy. These are false identifications that have nothing to do with them.

—Others are also I AM, God in active expression. The All-in-all expresses itself through them as good health, personal integrity, abundant supply, confidence, and joy.

---

78. *Jesus said, "Why have you come out into the desert? To see a reed shaken by the wind? And to see a man clothed in fine garments like your kings and your great men? Upon them are the fine garments, and they are unable to discern the truth." (No. 127)*

It is right for riches to belong to the children of light. It is possible, however, to be rich in money and goods and yet have nothing else to offer the world. Nor is it especially pleasant to associate with such people. As Jesus observed, "Upon them are the fine garments, and they are unable to discern the truth."

Matthew 11:7–8 and Luke 7:24–25 are parallel passages; in each gospel, the text continues with a reference to John the Baptist. This is probably the original context, for it was to see and hear John, and in many cases to be baptized, that city people came out into the desert. Jesus stated the contrast well: John was not at all like "a reed shaken by the wind." To the contrary, he was a strong and robust outdoor man, dressed in hides and brusque in manner. Although rough-hewn in his approach, he had a vital message—the coming of the kingdom of God.

The distinction between fine garments and being unable to discern the truth also has a deeper sense. The fine garments are a false belief system based on perceptual errors. Discerning the truth is their opposite, because it removes these false wraps from around one's consciousness. On another occasion, Jesus declared,

If you continue in my word *[en tō logō]*, you are truly my disciples, and you will know the truth, and the truth will make you free. (John 8:31–32)

AFFIRMATIONS

—I throw off old, wornout beliefs in error and limitation.
—I abide in the I AM, the Logos, the Cosmic Christ. I am open to receive God's perfect Ideas.
—I know the truth, and the truth has made me free.

---

79. *A woman from the crowd said to him, "Blessed are the womb which bore you and the breasts which nourished you."*

He said to her, "Blessed are those who have heard the word of the father and have truly kept it. For there will be days when you will say, 'Blessed are the womb which has not conceived and the breasts which have not given milk.'" (Nos. 236, 481)

The Gospel of Luke includes parallel passages, but in two segments:

As he said this, a woman in the crowd raised her voice and said to him, "Blessed is the womb that bore you, and the breasts that you sucked!" But he said, "Blessed rather are those who hear the word of God and keep it!"(Luke 11:27–28)

For behold, the days are coming when they will say, "Blessed are the barren, and the wombs that never bore, and the breasts that never gave suck!" (Luke 23:29)

The author of Thomas may have linked two originally independent sayings together as one. It is equally plausible, however, that the author of Luke split a unified source into two parts. In any case, the woman's seemingly tactless language was not so according to ancient conventions. She gave Jesus' mother a high compliment for bearing and raising such a fine son.

In the Jewish tradition it was, and still is, considered highly important for a woman to marry and to give birth to at least one child. If the children are male, so much the better. The achievements of an adult son bring honor to a Jewish woman. Jesus, in stating that it would be better to remain childless, did not speak in general terms. He referred rather to a given historical situation. He knew that the religious and governmental system of Judea was built on false foundations, and foresaw that it would be dismantled amid violence and suffering.

Jesus gave moral support to the institution of marriage, and was known as a friend and protector of children. He did, however, give primacy to the spiritual dimension of life. In this, Luke and Thomas fully agree. With minor variations, both record Jesus as praising those who hear the Word [Logos, Indwelling Christ] of God and maintain their attunement with It.

—I am open and receptive to the inspiration of the Indwelling Christ.
—I am attuned to the Divine guidance and ideas that I receive. I willingly listen and obey.

---

80. *Jesus said, "He who has recognized the world has found the body, but he who has found the body is superior to the world." (No. 296)*

This is an altered form of Saying 56. It now teaches "He (or she) who has recognized the world for what it is (using "world" in a negative sense) has found the body." As this suggests contempt for the body, the Coptic editor probably changed it. Again we find that the Egyptian version was not merely a translation, but in fact a new edition of the Gospel According to Thomas.

81. *Jesus said, "Let him who has grown rich be king, and let him who possesses power renounce it."*

Jesus used the analogy of a king in the parables of the Wedding Robe (Matt. 22:2, 11–13) and the King's Warfare (Luke 14:31–32). Discovering the formative power of thought is like becoming a king, with a real range of dominion. Quite appropriately, a popular writer of the early twentieth century, O. S. Marden, called one of his books *Every Man a King or Might in Mind-Mastery* (New York: Thomas Y. Crowell & Co., 1906).

"Growing rich" is here a symbol of awakening to the kingdom of God within. It means to identify with this expanded consciousness. This idea has affinities with Saying 76, which teaches, "Seek his unfailing and enduring treasure where no moth comes near to devour and no worm destroys."

Saying 81 ends with a paradox: "Let him who possesses power renounce it." We cannot abdicate the tendency of our thought to take form in the earth plane. It is an unfailing law, much as $2 + 2 = 4$, whether we like it or not. We can, however, shift our center of identity from the personal ego to the Indwelling Christ. We can trust and yield fully to the God within so that, on an individual level, we manifest the Oneness of Being rather than an illusory fragmentation of it. This trusting is to renounce power in the sense that Jesus intended.

AFFIRMATIONS

—I awaken to my true Self. I am rich in the Mind of Christ.
—It is not ego, but the God within, that does the work.

—I gladly yield my imperfect beliefs. I now receive the perfect wisdom of the Christ.

—As I grow in this perfect wisdom, health, harmony, and abundance flow into my experience.

---

82. *Jesus said, "He who is near me is near the fire, and he who is far from me is far from the kingdom."*

Origen, in his Homily on Jeremiah, quoted this statement but was uncertain about its authenticity. That it is a true saying of Jesus, however, is likely both by its content and its agreement with the Semitic literary tradition. Its key terms make it easy to remember, as is the case with many of Jesus' briefer sayings:

> near me / near the fire
> far from me / far from the kingdom

This form is known as *antithetic parallelism*. According to this structure, a positive statement precedes—or in some cases is followed by—a negative one that reinforces the positive. Antithetic parallelism is common in the Book of Proverbs; for example,

> A cheerful heart is a good medicine,
> but a downcast spirit dries up the bones.
> (Prov. 17:22)

Fire has a twofold symbology. First, it refers to purification. He who is near Jesus' state of consciousness will be purified of all thoughts and emotions that enslave, limit, or beset the individual. In the same sense, Malachi 3:2 states, "For he is like a refiner's fire and like fullers' soap." Malachi then presents the picture of a refiner of gold and silver, who burns away the dross so that the precious metal alone remains. Note also that when Jesus spoke of the Gehenna of fire, he did not refer to a place of punishment. He spoke of the Spirit's work in purifying the soul.

Second, fire refers to illumination, the realization of the Divine Presence. He who approaches Jesus' level of consciousness is near this fire. He who is far from Jesus' illumined state is far from the kingdom. In Mark 9:49, he affirms, "For every one will be salted with fire." Sooner or later, all will awaken to the kingdom of God that is within them.

AFFIRMATIONS

—The cleansing, healing, vitalizing Presence of God makes me whole and free.

—Peace fills my heart and mind. I am momently conscious of the Spirit's radiant Presence within me.

83. Jesus said, "The images are manifest to man, but the light in them remains concealed in the image of the light of the father. He will become manifest, but his image will remain concealed by his light."

Sayings 83–85 are among the most obscure in Thomas. They may record fragmentary notes of a class or discussion on the Book of Genesis, especially what we know today as Chapters 1–3. That Jesus gave such a class to his inner circle is, of course, possible.

Saying 83 begins with a contrast: (1) "the images [plural] that are manifest to man" and (2) "the image [singular] of the light of the Father." Philo of Alexandria (25 B.C. to A.D. 45) held that Genesis 1:2–3 refers to a spiritual creation in the realm of divine ideas and that Genesis 2:4–25 symbolizes the formation of the visible world. If this subject was being discussed by Thomas, the image of the light of the Father alludes to humankind being formed in the image of Elohim in Genesis 1:26–27. This image is the Word or Logos, including all the infinite ideas that inhere within It. Here is our eternal nature and Identity. By contrast, "the images that are manifest to man" are the images in the individual psyche that underlie the things and conditions that appear in time and space. These come and go, are subject to change, are formed and later stored away or erased.

A second contrast, also in Saying 83, offsets the terms manifest and concealed. It refers to the sense in which the visible universe, at the same time, both manifests and conceals the nature and potential of Infinite Mind. This paradox appears, for example, in Genesis 2:6: "A mist went up from the earth and watered the whole face of the ground." The Hebrew noun 'êd (a mist) can—as a footnote in the Revised Standard Version suggests—also mean "a flood." It can be taken either as an enveloping fog, or as a beneficial spring or flow to water the ground. Which, it has been asked, is true? Are the created earth in which we live, and the bodies we inhabit, a mist—a deceiving illusion? Or are they a flow of waters—a manifestation of God's perfect Mind? Neither statement is wholly true, or wholly false. The truth is found by going beyond the seeming contradiction to a larger view that includes both.

Many students have wracked their brains—or more precisely, the left sides of their brains—trying to reconcile this paradox. Others have argued, seriously and even vociferously, for one side or the other. What we must realize, first of all, is that the compiler of Genesis used paradox as a basic literary device. It is true that the Book of Genesis rests on earlier oral and written sources. Nevertheless, its editor had a style and personality of his own. Also, his success in using paradox to emphasize key issues is central to his literary genius.

The underlying purpose of paradox is to promote a shift of awareness, so that the reader or listener will be open to intuition. This is supported by modern psychoneurology, in its findings regarding the left and right hemispheres of the brain. The left hemisphere, with its analytical nature, declares, "It is either this way, or that." It cannot, of itself, do otherwise. The right hemisphere, however, can handle a *both / and* proposition, and see two sides of a paradox as parts of a larger whole. Gabriele Rico, a leading teacher of creative writing, states,

Since your Design mind [right hemisphere] is not constituted to see things as one way *or* the other, its predilection is always toward patterns; it focuses on complementarity rather than contradiction, on possible ways to connect opposites, to unify meaning. Thus it rejects the categories of either / or and accepts and plays with both / and. . . . To the Sign mind [left hemisphere] a polarity is the presence of two irreconcilable opposites. To the Design mind a polarity represents the ends of a single, indivisible whole. The focus is different, that's all, for it is the simultaneous recognition of opposites as equally valid.[1]

The allegories of Genesis still have significant teachings. In interpreting them, however, it is important to give primacy to their right-hemispheric contents. This is in accordance with the intent of the author—who thought in images more than in words—as well as with the metaphoric nature of the classical Hebrew language. The long-standing arguments between fundamentalists and modernists, as to the meaning of Genesis, have much to do with the *timing* of creation in the past. They have little or no relevance, however, to the mental and spiritual principles underlying God's creative action in the present. Time, we need to remember, is a left-hemispheric mental construct, not an objective fact. As such, these arguments have failed to address the central issues involved.

AFFIRMATIONS

—I am open and receptive to view the Scriptures in a new and fresh light.
—I love God with my mind, including both sides of my brain as an organ of its activity.
—I claim Divine inspiration as I read and study the Bible. All blocks to understanding are dissolved by the action of the Holy Spirit within me.

---

84. *Jesus said, "When you see your likeness, you rejoice. But when you see your images which came into being before you, and which neither die nor become manifest, how much you will have to bear!"*

"When you see your likeness, you rejoice." This probably refers to what is called the *energy body* or *etheric body.* It is the energy matrix that gives life, form, and function to the visible body. Once we become aware of its existence—whether through an out-of-body experience, or in some other way—we know that we are more than body, for we have consciously functioned apart from the physical brain. It is a reason to rejoice, because it means that we survive physical death.

"Your images which came into being before you, and which neither die nor become manifest," are Divine ideas. These eternal ideas, focused in the Cosmic Christ, underlie the existence of both the etheric body and, through its agency, of the visible side of our nature. They do not, however, manifest themselves *directly*, for they are not limited by human categories of time and space.

This second realization is greater than merely knowing the etheric body. We come to know that we are not only greater than our physical bodies, but also greater than our thoughts and emotions. We then identify with the Universal Consciousness. When we do so, our thoughts and emotions become clear channels of expression for our eternal Self. Our consciousness is transformed so that its contents facilitate the flow of Divine energy into harmonious form, instead of retarding it. Saying 85 affirms, in effect, that we shall awaken to our essential being, which can neither die nor be known directly through sensory channels.

AFFIRMATIONS

—I am greater than my body. I am also greater than my thoughts, for I am that which originates thought, God's perfect Idea.
—I AM; therefore, I think.
—I am free with the freedom of Spirit.
—I rejoice in the grace that makes me eternally one with All Good.

---

85. *Jesus said, "Adam came into being from a great power and a great wealth, but he did not become worthy of you. For had he been worthy, [he would] not [have experienced] death."*

Despite some missing words in the manuscript, a distinction between Adam and Jesus' disciples is obviously intended. This saying is closely related to the first-century concept of the First Adam and the Second Adam. Shifting to a metaphoric, right-hemispheric sense, we find that the two Adams represent two levels of consciousness. Some of Paul's statements are a variant of the same theme. For example, he affirmed,

But now is Christ risen from the dead, and become the firstfruits of them that slept. For since by man came death, by man came also the resurrection of the dead. For as in Adam all die, even so in Christ shall all be made alive. (1 Cor. 15:20–22, KJV)

The Hebrew word *adam* means "red; ruddy; a human being; a person of low degree." Here Adam represents the human body, which comes into being from the energy matrix mentioned in the previous commentary. This is, in a sense, "a great power and a great wealth."

The disciples, however, are called to advance beyond past limits and to show forth the Second Adam. Jesus called them to know and to identify with their Christ Self, which is also our spiritual calling today. This means a new birth, an inner realization of the kingdom of God. In Genesis 2:21, Adam falls asleep; the Scriptures do not really state that he ever awakened. It is possible, however, for us to awaken out of unconsciousness into our full Christ wisdom and dominion. When we do so, we become the "Second Adam," along with Jesus himself.

AFFIRMATIONS

—I am awakened out of human limitation, into my Christ nature and dominion.

—I am God's beloved son (daughter), in whom He is well pleased.

---

86. *Jesus said, "[The foxes have their holes] and the birds have [their] nests, but the son of man has no place to lay his head and rest." (No. 96)*

Matthew 8:20 and Luke 9:58 closely parallel this saying. The only substantive difference is that in Thomas, the phrase "and rest" appears at the end.

Many readers view these words as a lament over having no fixed and permanent home. This, however, is beside the point. The man mentioned in Matthew 8:19 and Luke 9:57 had offered to follow Jesus wherever he might go. Jesus wanted to test his commitment as a potential disciple. So he gave fair warning of the hardships of going with him on his travels. If he came along, there would be times when he would be hungry, thirsty, hot, cold, rained on, tired, and confronted by Jesus' enemies. It was no lifestyle for weaklings.

In addition, going with the Master has a deeper meaning of which physical travel is a metaphor. It is a moving into universal consciousness. Jesus' home is everywhere, because the Father is everywhere. The realization of the Divine Presence transcends time and space, being omnipresent in its scope. It is in this sense that Jesus "has no place to lay his head."

The various ways that the term "son of man" was used in ancient times is a complex historical issue. Its common usage in Aramaic, however, shows that it did not apply to Jesus alone. The expression referred to *any* human being, as contrasted to an angel on the one hand, and an animal on the other hand. Therefore, Saying 86 applies to us all. Whoever we are, contact with God is possible anywhere, at any time. We cannot be limited to a given place or system of ritual, unless we choose to limit ourselves.

"And rest" may or may not be part of the original saying. The source used by the authors of Matthew and Luke probably did not include this expression, but it may have been dropped at an earlier stage of transmission. In that case, the wording in Thomas would be original. On the other hand, the author of Thomas, or the Coptic editor, could have added it later.

The form in Thomas is at least plausible. The Odes of Solomon use the word *rest* in the sense of conscious oneness with God. For example, Ode 11:12 declares,

> And from above He gave me immortal rest,
> And I became like the land that blossoms
> and rejoices in its fruits.

AFFIRMATIONS

—I am always safe, secure, and at home in the loving, protecting Presence of God.

—I am poised and centered in the Christ Mind, and nothing can disturb the calm peace of my soul.

---

87. *Jesus said, "Wretched is the body that is dependent upon a body, and wretched is the soul that is dependent on these two."*

The following materials are all based on a common source or on closely related sources:

Matthew	8:19–20,	21–22
Luke	9:57–58,	59–60
Thomas	86,	87

And all three are close to Jesus' original "Saying 86." With Saying 87, however, the picture changes. Matthew and Luke are more original, although they contain a mistranslation from Aramaic into Greek. In its present form, Thomas contains not the saying itself but a grotesque attempt to interpret its meaning.

Matthew 8:21-22 reads,

Another of the disciples said to him, "Lord, let me first go and bury my father." But Jesus said to him, "Follow me, and leave the dead to bury their own dead."

People have sincerely asked, "Did Jesus recommend leaving dead bodies to rot in the open air?" Or still worse, "Did he expect corpses to rise up and bury another corpse?" No, he did not teach this. In Aramaic, which was Jesus' principal language, the word *metta* meant "dead," and the word *matta* meant "town." Evidently Jesus made a play on words that is clear in the original language but became confused in translation.

With this likely correction, the passage reads, "Leave the town to bury their own dead." He wanted to tell his prospective disciple to let the villagers perform this function; the urgency of his own mission had priority.

There are two reasons to conclude that the man's father had not actually died. First, to "go and bury my father" was an idiom meaning to care for an aged father who was still in the flesh. In the Aramaic culture, an elderly man who could no longer do useful work was, in a metaphoric sense, said to be "dead." Second, a funeral would only have taken a few days, and would not have been a serious obstacle to his joining with Jesus. Caring for his aged father over a period of years, however, was quite a different matter. It would have kept him at home until Jesus' earthly ministry was over, an irretrievable loss. Also, given Asian traditions of hospitality and of respect for elders, the villagers could reasonably have been expected to look after the old man's needs.

The original compiler of Thomas, who would have had to know Aramaic *and* Greek to complete his project, may well have understood the saying's original intent. This cannot, however, be said of an Egyptian who had only the Greek wording at his disposal. The work of the Coptic editor is thus clearly evident in Saying 87 as we have it in his text.

88. *Jesus said, "The angels and the prophets will come to you and give to you those things you (already) have. And you too, give them those things which you have, and say to yourselves, 'When will they come and take what is theirs?'"*

Although this saying may well be authentic, its Coptic text probably errs in placing the first sentence in the future tense. The Jews had had centuries of experience with angels and prophets (however one cares to define both), so this was nothing new. Also *in Aramaic there is no past or future. The tense of a sentence is taken from its context.* As a result, it is easy for tenses to be mistranslated.

In this case, angels appear to be a metaphor for human beings who are righteous or spiritually oriented. (This is also a proper metaphoric usage of the word "angel" in English.) Hebrews 13:1–2 advises, in a similar sense,

Let brotherly love continue. Do not neglect to show hospitality to strangers, for thereby some have entertained angels unawares.

Regarding prophets, it is true that many Jewish leaders in Jesus' time believed that the age of prophecy had ended. In so doing, however, they went against the tide both in Judaism itself and in the Greco-Roman world as a whole. Jesus, also, knew that the age of prophecy was still— and always will be—at least potentially present. For God is always the same.

"The angels and the prophets . . . give to you those things you (already) have." Read in the present tense, this is a basic insight not only into spiritual teaching but into *all* education. No one can really "bring" truth to us. They can only aid and inspire us to unfold our own innate knowledge and understanding. The very word *education* is from the Latin *educere,* which means "to lead forth from within." The best teachers in any field know how to do this. Other teachers, who lack this insight, remain mediocre despite their best efforts.

"And you too, give them those things which you have, and say to yourselves, 'When will they come and take what is theirs?' " If this educational principle applies when we are students, it applies equally when we are teachers. Also, Jesus taught his disciples that when they went out to teach others, as many of them would, they were to be more intent on giving of themselves than on receiving honors. By worldly standards, a person loses by giving. The realm of spiritual law, however, dictates the opposite. There is a way of giving that increases, and even multiplies, receiving. For example, Proverbs 11:24 reads,

> One man gives freely,
> yet grows all the richer;
> another withholds what he should give,
> and only suffers want.

In Luke 6:38, Jesus declares,

Give, and it will be given to you; good measure, pressed down, shaken together, running over, will be put into your lap. For the measure you give will be the measure you get back.

AFFIRMATIONS

—I recognize that all true learning is from the God within. Therefore, I am heir to all knowledge and understanding.

—There is no limit to what I can know, learn, and remember.

—I let go of all greed. I relax and rest in the peace of God.

—I give as the Holy Spirit guides me. I receive according to God's riches in glory in Christ Jesus.

---

89. *Jesus said, "Why do you wash the outside of the cup? Do you not realize that he who made the inside is the same one who made the outside?" (No. 187)*

The Gospel of Luke records similar words, but places them in a more definite setting. According to Luke 11:37–41 (see Matt. 23:25–26), they are addressed to the Pharisees, in a way that attacks their rules for the ceremonial washing of eating utensils:

[37]While he was speaking, a Pharisee asked him to dine with him; so he went in and sat at table. [38]The Pharisee was astonished to see that he did not first wash

before dinner. ³⁹And the Lord said to him, *"Now you Pharisees cleanse the outside of the cup* and of the dish, but inside you are full of extortion and wickedness. ⁴⁰You fools! *Did not he who made the outside make the inside also?* ⁴¹But give for alms those things which are within; and behold, everything is clean for you."

From a historical point of view, the setting in Luke is plausible but not necessarily original. Jesus could, of course, have made the statements in Saying 89 with reference to the Pharisees. It is false in *any* situation, however, to claim that actions alone are important and that thoughts are not. This has been called the "whited sepulchre" theory of religion, and for good reason.

Obviously, in a broader sense the meaning of Saying 89 extends beyond that of religious practices. The primacy of consciousness over action applies to all aspects of life; thus, in this saying, Jesus referred basically to the formative power of thought. The *inside* projects itself into visibility as the *outside*. In both, as he said, the activity of God is at work; that is, "he who made the inside is the same one who made the outside." As every cup by definition must have both an inside and an outside, or could not exist at all, so it is with all the facts and experiences of life.

Incidentally, a review of the Aramaic tradition clears up a discrepancy between Matthew 23:26 and Luke 11:41. Luke 11:41 (just shown) translates "give for alms," using a Greek term related to the English word *eleemosynary*. A similar statement in Matthew 23:26 declares, "First *cleanse [katharison*, related to the English word *catharsis]* the inside of the cup and of the plate, that the outside also may be clean." Here the author of Luke confused two Aramaic words, *dakkau* (to cleanse), and *zakkau* (to give alms). The correct word is *dakkau*, as shown in the Aramaic text of Matthew 23:26.

AFFIRMATIONS

—I am attuned to the Indwelling Christ.

—Through this attunement, I am transformed by the renewal of my mind.

—Inwardly and outwardly, I am healed, harmonized, and made whole.

---

90. *Jesus said, "Come unto me, for my yoke is easy and my lordship is mild, and you will find repose for youselves." (No. 134)*

The term *yoga*, which means union, is from the Sanskrit word for a yoke. In light of this ancient tradition, we find that the yoke that Jesus offers is conscious union with God. This union includes certain inner disciplines (yokes, yogas) that lead toward the goal. (The physical exercises and postures often associated with yoga in the western world are, more specifically, *hatha yoga*. They are only a minor part of the yogic systems and traditions of India.)

Certain scholars have concluded that Matthew 11:28–30 is actually an early Christian hymn. Not only is this statement correct, but we can now see that this section expands, in hymn form, Jesus' words as found in Thomas 90. Indeed, the invitation in 11:29 to "take my yoke upon you" means "Enter into the realization of Oneness with me." Also, when shown as poetry, Matthew 11:28–30 is suitable for liturgical use:

> Come to me, all who labor and are heavy laden,
> and I will give you rest.
> Take my yoke upon you, and learn from me;
> for I am gentle and lowly in heart,
> and you will find rest for your souls.
> For my yoke is easy, and my burden is light.

This section uses the same liturgical device as nine of the Odes of Solomon (see p. 13). That is, there is a shift from personal identity to identification with the Indwelling Christ. This means that the church in Antioch, of which the Gospel of Matthew is a product, was familiar with this liturgical form and presumably used it. It thus shows that this practice was not limited to the Odists themselves. The Antiochian Christians, as well as those of Eastern Syria, identified themselves with the Christ as an inner Reality and Principle.

The Odes of Solomon also use the symbol of the yoke. Ode 42 compares the yoke of union to "the arm of the bridegroom over the bride." In addition, this same ode proclaims "the yoke of my love." Oneness with God is thus referred to in intimate terms, and with an affirmation that the highest yoga is a consciousness of Divine Love. As in 1 John 4:8, "He who does not love does not know God; for God is love." Again, in 1 John 4:19, "We love, because he first loved us."

Ode 42:6–9 is written as from the mouth of Christ:

> Then I arose and am with them,
> And will speak by their mouths.
> For they have rejected those who persecute them;
> And I threw over them the yoke of my love.
> Like the arm of the bridegroom over the bride,
> So is my yoke over those who know me.
> And as the bridal feast is spread out by the bridal pair's home,
> So is my love by those who believe in me.

AFFIRMATIONS

—I am uplifted and encouraged by the realization that God is Love.

—I am one with the Love that is God.

—Light and joy and peace abide in me. My mind is poised in peace and beauty. I rest in calm trust, and rely on the Indwelling Christ to bring good into my experiences.

91. *They said to him, "Tell us who you are so that we may believe in you."*

He said to them, "You read the face of the sky and of the earth, but you have not recognized the one who is before you, and you do not know how to read this moment." (No. 151)

Many Jews, observing Jesus over a period of time, must have wondered whether he was the promised Messiah. In John 8:25, Jesus is asked the same question as in Thomas 91. Also, in Matthew 16:1, the Pharisees and Sadducees ask him for a sign in the sky. In effect, they challenged him to demonstrate his messiahship as they imagined that the true Messiah would do.

The example of "the face of the sky and of the earth" refers to trends in the weather, and the ability to forecast them. Sayings similar to those found in Matthew 16:2–3 (See Luke 12:54–55) still persist in rural areas. It is a fact that in most cases, a red sky in the evening will be followed by fair weather. If the sky is red in the morning, however, rain is likely.

The evidence shows that Jesus did not reply to his inquirers directly. *He wanted them to find the answer within themselves.* Thus he said, "Why do you not know how to interpret the present time?" (Luke 12:56). "You have not recognized the one who [can also be translated, that which] is before you, and you do not know how to read this moment" (Thom. 91). Jesus was the Messiah, it is true; but the inner Messiah or Christ was also within *them,* waiting to pour Its healing waters into their souls. He affirmed, in effect, "You are good at reading the surface appearances of earth and sky. You are less adept at knowing intuitively what is before you: The Cosmic Christ, and even the Omnipresence of God."

"Reading the present moment" could have referred in part to the developing political and religious crisis in Jerusalem. A common metaphor, "the signs of the times," is based on a related passage in Matthew 16:3. However, Jesus obviously had a broader meaning in mind. He referred to "reading" what mystics call the Eternal Now. This is also an experience that the individual must discover, as the Spirit within leads him or her to it. It is the realization that we are not in time, but in eternity. Time is a construct of personal thought, but eternity is the true nature of our being.

AFFIRMATIONS

—I am open to the Cosmic Christ as the healing, harmonizing, redeeming Center of my life.

—I awaken to the truth that eternity is now.

92. *Jesus said, "Seek and you will find. Yet, what you asked me about in former times and which I did not tell you then, now I do desire to tell, but you do not inquire after it." (No. 85)*

93. *Jesus said, "Do not give what is holy to dogs, lest they throw them on the dungheap. Do not throw the pearls [to] swine, lest they . . . it [. . .]." (No. 84)*

94. *Jesus [said], "He who seeks will find, and [he who knocks] will be let in." (No. 85)*

Sayings 92–94 include teachings also found in Matthew 7:6–8 and Luke 11:9–10. Except for the second sentence of Thomas 92, they apparently come from the same occasion in Jesus' teaching career:

TEACHINGS	THOMAS	MATTHEW	LUKE
Seek and you will find	92a	7:7	11:9
Do not give what is holy to dogs. . . . Do not throw the pearls to swine	93	7:6	—
He who seeks will find; he who knocks will be let in	94	7:8	11:10

Thomas 92b states, "Yet, what you asked me about in former times and which I did not tell you then, now I do desire to tell, but you do not inquire after it." This passage resembles John 16:4–5 enough to conclude that Jesus spoke in this manner at a later time, when his arrest and crucifixion were near. John 16:4–5 reads,

> But I have said these things to you, that when their hour comes you may remember that I told you of them. I did not say these thing to you from the beginning, because I was with you. But now I am going to him who sent me; yet none of you asks me, "Where are you going?"

The pair *"Seek and you will find"* / *"He who seeks will find"* reminds us that in the kingdom of God is an answer to every wholesome desire and a solution to every problem. The universe exists not to restrict us, but to meet our needs. The manner of seeking, however, determines the outcome. To seek for good only in worldly ways, apart from spiritual law, leads to failure and frustration. To seek in and from the Divine Source of all leads to success and fulfillment.

The pair *"Do not give what is holy to dogs"* / *"Do not throw the pearls to swine."* Several early Christian writers, including Clement of Alexandria and Origen, quoted this saying. To the Alexandrian School, it meant,

"Do not share secret teachings with those who are not ready for them."

With the Nuclear Age upon us, and its possibility of atomic warfare, the time for secrecy is past. The dangers of human ignorance are now greater than those that would result from scattered attempts to misuse mental laws. Even today, however, Jesus' saying has a valid application. We are not to share spiritual discoveries in an unwise manner, or press our points among people who would react with scorn. It is well, in every case, to seek Divine guidance in such matters.

AFFIRMATIONS

—I rejoice and give thanks that there is an answer to every need, and a solution to every problem.

—All my needs are met according to Divine Principle at work in my mind, body, and affairs.

---

95. *Jesus said, "If you have money, do not lend it at interest, but give [it] to one from whom you will not get it back." (No. 61)*

John Dominic Crossan lists this saying, as well as Matthew 5:42, Luke 6:30, and Didache 1:4–5 under the theme "Give Without Return." There is a point to generosity as a way of applying New Age understanding, for it can be an expression of the truth of universal supply. Also, to one who has become greedy or lives in a siege mentality, giving away money, land, and goods can have a healing effect on the giver, as well as benefiting others.

It is difficult, however, to believe that Jesus declared against lending money at interest. The Parable of the Hidden Treasure in Thomas 109 concludes with the statement "He began to lend money at interest to whomever he wished." And in two other parables he is critical of a man who *fails* to do so:

Then you ought to have invested my money with the bankers, and at my coming I should have received what was my own with interest. (Matt. 25:27, Parable of the Talents)

Why then did you not put my money into the bank, and at my coming I should have collected it with interest? (Luke 19:23, Parable of the Pounds)

Receiving a commercial loan is often an answer to prayer, enabling an entrepreneur to carry out a God-inspired idea. When this is done, many other people become gainfully employed and the general public also benefits. For this and other reasons, credit has a legitimate function in the business world.

96. *Jesus said, "The kingdom of the father is like [a certain] woman. She took a little leaven, [concealed] it in some dough, and made it into large loaves. Let him who has ears hear." (Nos. 4, 130)*

This is a variant of the Parable of the Leaven, also found in Matthew 13:33 and Luke 13:20–21. No doubt Jesus gave many of his parables more than once, with differences in detail.

The woman is an archetypal symbol of the soul, especially on the level of deep-seated beliefs, attitudes, and emotional patterns. The leaven is the Holy Spirit, active on a subconscious level. All real improvement in life requires subconscious change, which the God within makes possible.

Leaven acts in bread silently and also invisibly, yet with great energy. Similarly, the healing of the psyche works silently. Also, we do not see Spirit with our physical eyes, but we experience Its Presence and Power within us in unmistakable ways. Also, we show forth the results of this action as applied intelligence, a healthy body, and harmonious progress in the affairs of life.

AFFIRMATIONS

—I welcome the leaven of the Holy Spirit within me. I am permeated and penetrated by Divine ideas active within my soul and body.

—I rejoice in the victory of God's truth, life, love, and joy within me and my experience.

---

97. *Jesus said, "The kingdom of the [father] is like a certain woman who was carrying a [jar] full of meal. While she was walking [on the] road, still some distance from home, the handle of the jar broke and the meal emptied out behind her [on] the road. She did not realize it; she had noticed no accident. When she reached her house, she set the jar down and found it empty."*

Only the Gospel of Thomas preserves the Parable of the Jar. However, a second-century work called the Gospel of Truth refers to it. A section on "The Anointing" begins thus:

> The anointing is the mercy of the Father with which He will have mercy on them. And those whom he has anointed, they are complete. For it is the full jars that are wont to be anointed. But when the anointing of one jar shall be destroyed, it is wont to leak. And the reason why it shall lack content is the fact that its anointing shall depart from it.[1]

In the Parable of the Leaven (Thomas 96), the end result would be to eat the bread. This eating represents the assimilation of Divine ideas—such as life, truth, and love—into consciousness. In the Parable of the Jar, the opposite occurs. The meal is lost, so that there is none left to bake into bread and eat.

The woman is again a symbol of the soul, here walking the path of life. The parable is factual, for in the traditional Near East women carry jars containing water or meal. The meal is ground from seeds, which represent Divine ideas. She loses the meal gradually and without her notice. Therefore, she symbolizes an attitude in which one's true purpose in life is ignored or forgotten. As a result, spiritual progress fails to occur.

Many people begin life with great promise. Yet at the end of earth life, they find spiritual growth unattained and hopes unfulfilled. "The saddest words of tongue and pen are still, 'It might have been!'" It behooves us, therefore, to seek Divine guidance as to our true work and purpose in life.

AFFIRMATIONS

—I seek God's plan and purpose for my life. Father, I will go where you want me to go. I will be what you want me to be.

—I accept and receive the anointing of the Holy Spirit.

---

98. *Jesus said, "The kingdom of the father is like a certain man who wanted to kill a powerful man. In his own house he drew his sword and stuck it into the wall in order to find out whether his hand could carry through. Then he slew the powerful man."*

This parable is also found only in Thomas. The sword represents the Word or Logos in its active aspect of overcoming its seeming opposite. The hand is a symbol of executive ability, especially the power of an idea to extend itself into action. This use of the sword image has affinities with Hebrews 4:12 and Ephesians 6:17, quoted in connection with Saying 16.

The Gospel of Truth alludes to Sayings 97 and 98 in a section called "Jars and Judgment." Either the author borrowed from the Gospel of Thomas (the more likely choice), or else both writers drew from a common tradition that included both parables. The Gospel of Truth here freely adapts the image of the jar. However, it mentions the sword in the same sense as in the parable and in the New Testament: "Being a drawn sword of two edges cutting this way and that: when came into the midst the Word who is in the heart of those who speak it."[1]

According to the parable, the Christian warrior is to conquer error (*planē* in the New Testament) in two steps: (1) in her or his individual psyche and (2) in the collective belief system of the planet. The man's first step is to drive the sword into the wall of his house; that is, into *his own* consciousness. Once our attunement with the Indwelling Christ is stabilized, however, we can help to bring healing and illumination to the whole human race. This is represented by using the sword to slay the strong man who, as in Saying 35, is a symbol of collective error. This collective image of evil and negation will ultimately be destroyed, root and branch, through the power of the Christ, the Word of God.

—I rejoice that the Sword of the Spirit, the Indwelling Christ, destroys all that is unlike Itself.

—I rejoice that God the Good is the only Creative Mind, the only creative action, and the only creation.

---

99. *The disciples said to him, "Your brothers and your mother are standing outside."*

He said to them, "Those here who do the will of my father are my brothers and my mother. It is they who will enter the kingdom of my father." (No. 435)

Jesus expanded the meaning of *family* to include all those who shared his attunement with the Infinite, or at least aspired to do so. He wanted to break down narrow, exclusive barriers that separated families from one another. He saw universal love and brotherhood as a possible and even inevitable goal. We find similar words in Matthew 12:46–50, Mark 3:31–35, Luke 8:19–21, 2 Clement 9:11, and the Gospel of the Ebionites as quoted by Epiphanius.

Jesus' mother and brothers, and also some friends, worried about him. The Marcan text implies a long and strenuous period of activity, to which there seemed to be no end.

Then he went home; and the crowd came together again, so that they could not even eat. And when his family heard it, they went out to seize him, for people were saying, "He is beside himself." (Mark 3:19–21)

Despite their worry, he did not take a rest as they wanted. He was human enough to get tired and sleep through a storm (Mark 4:38). Yet he apparently had great reserves of energy that kept him going when most men would falter. Also, though in some sense "beside himself," his family and friends were not in a position to pass judgment on his altered state of consciousness (which the Greek text implies).

Friendships based on spiritual oneness can be more enduring than those based on blood or marriage. Relationships in this world come and go, but our oneness in Christ is forever. When we are in tune with what Jesus calls "the kingdom of my father," and others are also, they become to us as our brother, and sister, and mother.

AFFIRMATIONS

—I am free from biases about age, sex, race, and social class.

—I am willing to accept both myself and others as children of God.

—I realize that in Christ, I am one with all people, and all people are one with me.

—I attract friends who share my interests.
—To have friends, I am willing to be a friend to others.

---

100. *They showed Jesus a gold coin and said to him, "Caesar's men demand taxes from us."*
He said to them, "Give Caesar what belongs to Caesar, give God what belongs to God, and give me what is mine." (No. 454)

This saying is based on an authentic tradition, but bears little resemblance to the original. Its background was the levying of taxes by the Roman government in Palestine. Matthew 22:15–22, Mark 12:13–17, and Luke 20:19–26 point to the importance of this issue at the time. Saying 100, then, refers to an attempt to trap Jesus by the question "Is it lawful to pay taxes to Caesar, or not?" (Matt. 22:17 and Mark 12:14; see also Luke 20:22).

If Jesus had said, "It is not lawful," he would have been a revolutionary from the Roman point of view. If he had said, "It is lawful," he would have alienated many of the common people, most of whom did not pay taxes to Caesar. They avoided the annual "head tax" by refusing to use Roman coinage, and there were too many of them for the Romans to try more than a token enforcement. Note that these coins bore the image of whoever was emperor at the time of issue. The emperors believed themselves to be divine, and demanded worship. As a result, the Jews considered Roman money to be contrary to the Second Commandment, which forbids graven images.

Jesus' answer was "Render to Caesar the things that are Caesar's, and to God the things that are God's" (Mark 12:17 and parallels). This reply was remarkably astute. From the Roman point of view, he voiced approval of giving taxes to Caesar. To his loyal hearers, however, this was not a true concession. As already noted, they did not use Roman money, and therefore did not pay the tax in any case. He knew it, and they knew it. Let us not, then, give undue weight to the call to "give Caesar his due." According to Jesus' frame of reference—which this incident, correctly understood, does not negate—*all things are God's.*

The form of Saying 100 differs from the other evidence. For it claims that Jesus divided life into three spheres: those of the political state, God, and himself. The claim that God and Jesus have separate spheres coincides with a later view held in the second century. Marcion and others believed that the Creator God of the Jews was a different deity from the God whom Jesus came to reveal. They claimed that Jesus had not been born of Mary, but had arrived as a full-grown man from somewhere outside the created universe. This notion amounts to a pre-Copernican form of science fiction. It is a clue to the belief system of the Coptic editor, who almost certainly tampered with this account.

101. *Jesus said, "Whoever does not hate his [father] and his mother as I do cannot become a [disciple] to me. And whoever does [not] love his [father and] his mother as I do cannot become a disciple to me. For my mother . . . but [my] true [mother] gave me life." (No. 121)*

This saying has some gaps in its manuscript. The bracketed words are educated guesses by the translator. Also, the partial parallel to Saying 55 shows that the word translated "hate" is to be traced back to an Aramaic term that also means "put aside." There are, it is true, situations where grown people have to put their parents aside out of loyalty to a higher principle. Yet hatred of parents cannot be condoned. It is inconsistent with the nature of God, who is Love.

The heart of the original saying is a contrast between human parents and God as our Divine Parent. It also affirms that the metaphors of Father and Mother are equally valid in talking of God. Our Divine Source is not only the progenitor of our being but also its continuing nourishment and support. God is Wisdom, but God is also—to repeat—Love. This agrees with the fact that the Hebrew word for Spirit, *ruah,* is in the feminine gender.

The Odes of Solomon also affirms the idea of God as both Father and Mother. Ode 19:1–2 includes analogies that are curious by modern standards:

> A cup of milk was offered to me,
> And I drank it in the sweetness of the Lord's kindness.
> The Son is the cup,
> And the Father is He who was milked;
> And the Holy Spirit is She who milked Him.

God is both She and He according to Ode 36:1,5:

> I rested on the Spirit of the Lord,
> And She lifted me up to heaven; . . .
> For according to the greatness of the Most High, so She made me;
> And according to His newness He renewed me.

AFFIRMATIONS

—I rejoice in the vision that God is my Mother and my Father.

—God is Wisdom; therefore I am wise. I express wisdom in thought, word, and action.

—God is Love; therefore I am loving. I express love in thought, word, and action.

102. *Jesus said, "Woe to the pharisees, for they are like a dog sleeping in the manger of oxen, for neither does he eat nor does he [let] the oxen eat." (No. 181)*

Aesop (approximately 620–560 B.C.), the Greek storyteller, used the dog in the manger in one of his fables. It is quite possible, however, that Jesus adapted this image to serve his own purpose. The dog who does not eat, nor let the oxen eat, is a graphic way of expressing the point of Thomas 39a (see Matt. 23:13; Luke 11:52):

> The Pharisees and the scribes have taken the keys of knowledge and hidden them. They themselves have not entered, nor have they allowed to enter those who wish to.

103. *Jesus said, "Fortunate is the man who knows where the brigands will enter, so that [he] may get up, muster his domain, and arm himself before they invade." (No. 206)*

This is another version of the Simile of the Burglar. Unlike Thomas 21, Matthew 24:43, and Luke 12:39, no context is given. See the earlier commentary on Thomas 21.

104. *They said to Jesus, "Come, let us pray today and let us fast."*
Jesus said, "What is the sin that I have committed, or wherein have I been defeated? But when the bridegroom leaves the bridal chamber, then let them fast and pray." (No. 331)

This is similar to Matthew 9:14–15, Mark 2:18–20, and Luke 5:33-35. The Lucan account reads,

> And they said to him, "The disciples of John fast often and offer prayers, and so do the disciples of the Pharisees, but yours eat and drink." And Jesus said to them, "Can you make wedding guests fast while the bridegroom is with them? The days will come, when the bridegroom is taken away from them, and then they will fast in those days."

Weddings are occasions for great feasting in the traditional Near East. The fasting comes later, after the feast. Jesus and his disciples feasted as a celebration of the kingdom of God in their midst. The outer feast was a parable of action, expressing the joy of their inner feast on Divine ideas.

As in Saying 75, entering the bridal chamber is another metaphor for entering the inner kingdom. The Indwelling Christ and the soul are wedded in the realization of Oneness.

AFFIRMATIONS

—I am not limited to the outer channels of sense. I continually feast on divine ideas, and I am renewed and made whole.

—I celebrate life. I celebrate wholeness. I celebrate the unlimited Mind of Christ.

---

105. *Jesus said, "He who knows the father and the mother will be called the son of a harlot."*

In John 8:41, Jesus' adversaries made the snide remark: "We were not born of fornication." Jesus replied,

> If God were your Father, you would love me, for I proceeded and came forth from God; . . . But you have not known him; I know him. (John 8:42,55)

Saying 105 records the irony of Jesus' retort more clearly. His critics had the audacity to denounce Mary as a fornicator, or even as a whore. Yet Jesus knew his Father-Mother God, and his opponents did not. They were the spiritual bastards who did not know their true Parent. Their fixation on human ancestry had blinded them to the fact that they, too, were sons of God.

106. *Jesus said, "When you make the two one, you will become the sons of man, and when you say, 'Mountain, move away,' it will move away." (Nos. 293, 345, 452)*

Saying 106 has certain affinities with Thomas 22, 30, and 48. First, the image *"When you make the two one"* can again be taken on several levels. In the present context, it has to do at least partly with healing inner conflicts. As regarding Saying 22: "The mind and the heart, logic and intuition, are reconciled from a higher level." With our willingness, the Indwelling Christ can redeem and activate both the left and right hemispheres of the brain, and normalize the interaction between them. As this is accomplished, we are able to release our full potential; that is, to "become the sons of man."

"And when you say, 'Mountain, move away,' it will move away"—when thought and feeling agree, positive action and practical demonstration follow. Changing one's conscious thinking does not, in and of itself, produce change. When the subconscious mind accepts the new thought or image or belief pattern, *then* change is certain—for the two (thought and feeling) have been made one.

Modern psychoneurology has shown that the right hemisphere of the brain generally functions as the doorway to the subconscious mind. Therefore, increasing left-right cerebral interaction makes it easier to reprogram the subconscious mind in a positive direction.

AFFIRMATIONS

—I am willing for all blocks to be removed to the realization of Divine Love.

—God is Love, God is Peace, active in me now.

—God is Love, God is Peace, active in all people and in all creatures.

—I am unified, harmonized, and attuned to the One Presence and One Power, God the Good, All-governing.

---

107. *Jesus said, "The kingdom is like a shepherd who had a hundred sheep. One of them, the largest, went astray. He left the ninety-nine and looked for that one until he found it. When he had gone to such trouble, he said to the sheep, 'I care for you more than the ninety-nine.' " (No. 8)*

The Parable of the Lost Sheep is also found in Matthew 18:12–13 and Luke 15:4–6. The Gospel of Truth mentions it, too. Although it can be interpreted on several levels, two are readily apparent. In one sense, Jesus himself is the Good Shepherd. He goes out to seek those who are mentally, morally, and spiritually lost. He is a vehicle of God's action in seeking out fallen humanity, to return them to the "sheepfold" of God's healing and protecting love.

In another sense, the I AM or Indwelling Christ is the Good Shepherd. The Christ in us shepherds our thoughts, emotions, and beliefs. When we become aware of a "dark" area of our psyche, we bring the I AM to bear on it, so that the negative factor is transformed into a positive one. The sheep that receives the shepherd's special care is an error thought that is transmuted into a true thought. In many cases, one's former weakness is changed into one's greatest strength. As Kathryn Jarvis said, "No one is stronger than a timid man who has overcome his timidity."[1]

AFFIRMATIONS

—I rejoice that before I call, God has answered. We seek God because he first seeks us. Praise God who is Love, Joy, and Peace.

—I AM is the Good Shepherd. I am shown what is positive and good in thought, feeling, word, and action.

—The Light of God within me transforms darkness into light, and I know the way.

---

108. *Jesus said, "He who will drink from my mouth will become like me. I myself shall become he, and the things that are hidden will be revealed to him."*

To "drink from my mouth" means to receive Truth direct from the Word or Indwelling Christ (see Thom. 13). John 4:14, in a similar sense, affirms that "whoever drinks of the water that I [Jesus] shall give him will never thirst; the water that I shall give him will become in him a spring of water welling up to eternal life." In John 7:37–38, Jesus refers to "rivers of living water" that flow out from within. Revelation 22:17 gives the invitation: "Let him who is thirsty come, let him who desires take the water of life without price."

The Odes of Solomon 12:1–3 gives an especially close parallel of thought and imagery:

> He has filled me with words of truth,
> That I may proclaim Him.
> And like the flowing of waters, truth flows from my mouth,
> And my lips declare His fruits.
> And He has caused His knowledge to abound in me,
> Because the mouth of the Lord is the true Word,
> And the entrance of His light.

AFFIRMATIONS

—I do not live by bread alone, but by every idea that inheres in the Mind of God.

—I am transformed and renewed by the flow of living waters within my soul and body.

---

109. *Jesus said, "The kingdom is like a man who had a [hidden] treasure in his field without knowing it. And [after] he died, he left it to his [son]. The son [did] not know (about the treasure). He inherited the field and sold [it]. And the one who bought it went plowing and [found] the treasure. He began to lend money at interest to whomever he wished." (No. 5)*

This version of the Parable of the Hidden Treasure is quite different from that in Matthew 13:44:

> The kingdom of heaven is like treasure hidden in a field, which a man found and covered up; then in his joy he goes and sells all that he has and buys that field.

The hidden treasure is the Presence and Power of God, who lives in all of us. The biblical version has basically the same meaning as the Pearl (Matt. 13:45–46; Thom. 76) and the Great Fish (Thom. 8). In all three, the person gives up everything else to obtain the treasure, the pearl, or the fish. This means that all former viewpoints are let go in order to unite with the Indwelling Christ, and to live with the realization of one Presence and one Power.

In Saying 109, which is an entirely separate parable, the treasure is still the Divine Presence. Likewise, finding the treasure represents its discovery within us. However, the image of lending money at interest gives it a different emphasis. It reminds us that Jesus is the practical mystic, who makes outer demonstrations of inward Truth. The man who finds the treasure does what the third servant in the Parable of the Talents fails to do. Matthew 25:24–27 reads,

> He also who had received the one talent came forward, saying, "Master, I knew you to be a hard man, reaping where you did not sow, and gathering where you did not winnow; so I was afraid, and I went and hid your talent in the ground. Here you have what is yours." But his master answered him, "You wicked and slothful servant! You knew that I reap where I have not sowed, and gather where I have not winnowed? Then you ought to have invested my money with the bankers, and at my coming I should have received what was my own with interest."

In Thomas 109, the owner discovers the treasure while plowing. As in the Wheat and the Tares (Matt. 13:24–30; Thom. 57) and the Seed Growing Secretly (Mark 4:26–29), the ground represents the subconscious mind. Thus, while probing the subconscious has its limitations and its risks, one who does so has a reasonable chance of reaching deeper to the Superconscious level where the hidden treasure lies.

Lending out money at interest also draws a parallel between the world of finance and the hidden realms of thought: *Use is the law of increase.* We increase any quality or skill by imaging it, and then expressing it in practical ways. This is true even of spiritual qualities, such as love, wisdom, joy, and peace.

AFFIRMATIONS

—I joyfully awaken to the inner Treasure, the Presence and Power of God.

—I abide continually in the Indwelling Spirit of God. As I do so, harmony, order, and fulfillment are brought into my affairs.

—I am inspired to know how to apply the laws of the kingdom in orderly and practical ways.

---

110. *Jesus said, "Whoever finds the world and becomes rich, let him renounce the world."*

This saying is somewhat like Thomas 81, which reads, "Let him who has grown rich be king, and let him who possesses power renounce it."

"Whoever finds the world" is one who can identify his or her own errors and misperceptions, and thus see beyond them to the truth. To become rich is again a symbol of discovering the Christ Mind within, with its unlimited richess of divine ideas.

"Let him renounce the world." Jesus is saying, "Having discerned the difference between the real and the counterfeit, the true and the false, let him or her renounce the errors of sin, disease, ignorance, and lack.

Let him or her claim the integrity, wholeness, wisdom, and abundance of Spirit."

The Odes of Solomon also identify "the world" with worldly thought, rather than with a geographical place:

> I am a priest of the Lord,
> And Him I serve as a priest;
> And to Him I offer the offering of His thought.
> For His thought is not like the world,
> Nor like the flesh,
> Nor like them who worship according to the flesh.
> The offering of the Lord is righteousness,
> And purity of heart and lips.
>
> (Ode 20:1–4)

AFFIRMATIONS

—I renounce all errors based on the illusion of God's absence. I affirm the All-presence of God, available to meet every need.

—I claim the integrity, wholeness, wisdom, and abundance of Spirit. This is my Divine inheritance as a son (daughter) of God.

---

111. *Jesus said, "The heavens and the earth will be rolled up in your presence. And the one who lives from the living one will not see death." Does not Jesus say, "Whoever finds himself is superior to the world?" (No. 278)*

These are really three separate sayings, and it is best to review them as such.

"The heavens and the earth will be rolled up in your presence." This sentence dramatizes the passing away of an illusory belief system, together with its negative results. The image of the old heaven and earth passing away, to be replaced by a new order, has roots in Isaiah 34:4 and 54:10. In the New Testament, Revelation 21:1–4 and 2 Peter 3:10–13 directly announce the new heaven and the new earth. My commentary on Thomas 11 also applies to this teaching.

In addition, Hebrews 1:10–12 (New English Bible) reads like an expansion of the first sentence of Saying 111. It also includes the related images of the old and new garments:

> By thee, Lord, were earth's foundations laid of old,
> and the heavens are the work of thy hands.
> They shall pass away, but thou endurest;
> like clothes they shall all grow old;
> thou shalt fold them up like a cloak;
> yes, they shall be changed like any garment.
> But thou art the same, and thy years shall have no end.

"The one who lives from the living one will not see death." Whoever lives in and from the Christ Presence will not view life in terms of sin, disease, and death. He or she will live with a realization of eternal life, here and now. He or she will look forward to an eternal unfoldment of what is good. Hour by hour, such a person will live in conscious union with God, which is our natural state.

"Whoever finds himself is superior to the world." This correlates closely with Saying 3 (Greek edition), which affirms in part: *The kingdom is within you, and when you know yourselves you will find it.* Whoever finds his or her true Self, the "I AM" or Christ, has dominion over all worldly thoughts and conditions.

AFFIRMATIONS

—All false thoughts and conditions are dissolved in the living Presence of God.

— The Indwelling Christ works powerfully in my consciousness. A new attitude and a new heart have been prepared for me. Life, love, joy, and peace now flow into my experience.

—I live from the Living One within me. I think from the Living One within me. I prevail through the Living One within me.

—I am the Living One in active expression. I know it, I feel it, and I demonstrate it.

—The Indwelling Christ has abolished death and brought life and immortality to light in my experience.

---

112. *Jesus said, "Woe to the flesh that depends on the soul; woe to the soul that depends on the flesh."*

Regarding the original form of this saying, only an educated guess is possible. We have noted that Jesus sometimes used the couplet form. What we have here, however, is two woes. If we take the example of Luke 6:20–26, every woe is the reverse side of a blessing. To be specific:

> Blessed are you poor/Woe to you that are rich
> Blessed are you that hunger now/Woe to you that are full now
> Blessed are you that weep now/Woe to you that laugh now
> Blessed are you when men hate you/Woe to you, when all men
> speak well of you

Accordingly, Saying 112 may have originally read

> *Blessed* is the flesh that depends on the soul;
> woe to the soul that depends on the flesh.

In this form, the couplet does not affirm a neurotic opposition of soul and body. Rather, line 1 suggests the idea of healing the body through an inner change of consciousness. Line 2 implies that we are to welcome our intuitive awareness, and not become unduly dependent on sensory channels ("the flesh") for our understanding of life.

As given in the Coptic text, Saying 112 teaches that soul and body—and by extension, the inner consciousness and the outer world—are basically hostile. Jesus, however, saw life as a parable, with the inner and the outer facts of life parallel to each other.

113. *His disciples said to him, "When will the kingdom come?"*

Jesus said, "It will not come by waiting for it. It will not be a matter of saying, 'here it is' or 'there it is.' Rather, the kingdom of the father is spread out upon the earth, and men do not see it." (No. 196)

The kingdom, as Jesus says here, is not only within our consciousness (see Luke 17:21, Thom. 3). It is also spread out upon the earth, indwelling everyone and everything. The earth is a great eucharist, filled with the substance and life of the Spirit, when we are able to see it as such. The key is not to wait passively for the kingdom's coming, but to awaken to its reality here and now. As Jesus also declares in Saying 51, "What you look forward to has already come, but you do not recognize it."

To summarize, Jesus' statements in Luke 17:21 and Thomas 3 correlate well with Thomas 51 and 113. When we find the realm of divine ideas within, we then also view the earth through different eyes. What was once dead and mechanical becomes full of light and vitality. Our struggle toward light and liberty is changed into the realization that we are the light and liberty we seek. When our consciousness is transformed, our experience of the outer world is transformed along with it.

AFFIRMATIONS

—I awaken into the consciousness of the Spirit of God in me.

—Whatever I need is prepared and available through the Spirit of God in me. I now claim it, in faith and trust.

—I awaken to the kingdom of the Father, which is even now spread out upon the earth.

—There is one Mind and one Substance, that now reveals itself in ways both invisible and visible.

---

114. *Simon Peter said to them, "Let Mary leave us, for women are not worthy of life."*

Jesus said, "I myself shall lead her in order to make her male, so that she too may become a living spirit resembling you males. For every woman who will make herself male will enter the kingdom of heaven."

The statement attributed to Peter is fictional, and should be discounted. We noted in connection with Saying 61 that *Salome* sometimes appeared in spiritual dialogues as a literary device. The same applies to Mary Magdalene, whose name is variously known as Mary, Mariham, and Mariamne. The Pistis Sophia, Acts of Philip, and Gospel of Mary all have this feature. In fact, in the last work Mary holds forth as a revealer of mysteries.

Although the words here ascribed to Jesus are probably not genuine, neither are they as antiwomen as they appear. In some circles, a woman symbolized a purely human level of consciousness, whereas a man represented a divine level of knowing (attainable by members of both sexes). Ignatius, a bishop of Syrian Antioch, wrote early in the second century, "Let me receive pure light. When I do so, I shall indeed become a man" (Ign. Romans 6:2). Also, the statement that "I myself shall lead her . . . so that she too may become a living spirit" is consonant with 1 Corinthians 6:17, which reads, "He who is united to the Lord becomes one spirit with him."

In the Gospel of Mary, also found in the Nag Hammadi collection, Mary declares, "Let us praise his greatness, for he has prepared us and made us into men."[1] This is obviously not intended literally, but rather, figuratively.

In light of the symbology suggested here, Saying 114 affirms,

> I myself [the Indwelling Christ]
> shall lead her [the soul]
> in order to make her male [spiritually illumined] . . .
> For every woman [soul]
> who makes herself male [spiritually illumined]
> will enter the kingdom of heaven.

In the Divine Plan, women and men are not meant to be in conflict, but to complement one another. Members of both sexes share the capacity to grow both in reason and in intuition. Both, also, have the same dignity as the image of God, and share equal access to the kingdom.

AFFIRMATIONS

—My soul is illumined by Spiritual Man, the Christ.

—My confidence in life is restored, because I am awake in God, the Source and Substance of all life.

Epilogue

―――――――

The greatest value of the Gospel of Thomas is that it can help us capture Jesus' New Age vision of Reality. When we do so, we are in turn captured by that vision and progressively transformed by it. In our own everyday lives, we fulfill the promise of 2 Corinthians 3:17–18, which declares,

Now the Lord is the Spirit, and where the Spirit of the Lord is, there is freedom. And we all, with unveiled face, beholding the glory of the Lord, are being changed into his likeness from one degree of glory to another; for this comes from the Lord who is the Spirit.

Notes

INTRODUCTION
1. James M. Robinson, ed., *The Nag Hammadi Library* (San Francisco: Harper & Row, 1977), p. 1. See Robinson's Introduction for background information on the Nag Hammadi Library.
2. *Biblical Archeologist,* 1979, article by James M. Robinson entitled "Introduction: What is the Nag Hammadi Library?", pp. 201–2.
3. Twelve of the *parables* of Jesus found in Matthew, Mark, and Luke appear also in Thomas, together with three that are entirely new to our knowledge. Though translated from Aramaic (the language of Jesus' parables), and then from Greek, the parables in Thomas are otherwise close to their original form, and are a significant factor in the field of parables research.

    In *The Fifth Gospel,* I have decided to keep my comments on the parables brief. A subject of this scope calls for more thorough treatment than is practical in a work on the Gospel of Thomas as a whole. In a forthcoming work, *The God Within,* I provide a thorough review of the parables, including those in Thomas.
4. Robinson, p. 117.
5. See Robert Winterhalter, *The Odes of Solomon: Original Christianity Revealed* (St. Paul, MN: Llewellyn, 1985).

PREFACE
1. Robinson, *The Nag Hammadi Library,* p. 189.

SAYING 2
1. Matthew Black, *An Aramaic Approach to the Gospels and Acts,* 3rd ed. (Oxford: Oxford University Press, 1967), p. 143.

SAYING 16
1. Black, p. 155.

SAYING 22
1. George Lamsa, *More Light on the Gospel* (Garden City, NY: Doubleday, 1968), p. 6.

SAYING 32
1. Jack Finegan, *Hidden Records of the Life of Jesus* (Philadelphia: Pilgrim Press, 1969), p. 250.

SAYING 33
1. M. Marcovich, "Textual Criticism of the Gospel of Thomas," *The Journal of Theological Studies* (Oxford at the Clarendon Press), 1969, *20*, p. 55.

SAYING 44
1. Bernard B. Scott, *Jesus, Symbol-Maker for the Kingdom* (Philadelphia: Fortress Press, 1981), p. 166.

SAYING 52
1. D. R. A. Hare, "The Lives of the Prophets," in James H. Charlesworth, ed., *The Old Testament Pseudepigrapha*, Vol. 2 (Garden City, N.Y.: Doubleday, 1985), pp. 380–81.
2. Hare, pp. 385–399.

SAYING 54
1. Emmet Fox, *The Sermon on the Mount* (New York: Harper & Row, 1934), p. 22.

SAYING 60
1. *Metaphysical Bible Dictionary*, (Lee's Summit, MO: Unity School of Christianity, 1931), p. 568.

SAYINGS 65–66
1. John Dominic Crossan agrees with this conclusion, which he discusses in his book, *In Parables* (San Francisco: Harper & Row, 1973), pp. 86–96.

SAYING 77
1. M. R. James, *The Apocryphal New Testament* (Oxford at the Clarendon Press, 1924), p. 335.
2. Robinson, p. 38.

SAYING 83
1. Gabriele Lusser Rico, *Writing the Natural Way* (Los Angeles: Tarcher, 1983), p. 212.

SAYING 97
1. Kendrick Grobel, trans., *The Gospel of Truth* (Nashville: Abingdon Press, 1955), pp. 168, 170.

SAYING 98
1. Grobel, p. 104.

SAYING 107
1. Kathryn Jarvis taught spiritual counseling at Unity School of Christianity in the early 1960s. This quotation is from my class notes.

SAYING 114
1. Robinson, p. 472.

Cross-References to the Bible

This appendix lists all the Bible references mentioned in *The Fifth Gospel*, except for the Epilogue. Verses that are included in the text itself, in whole or in part, are shown in italics. Numbers in brackets refer to Sayings numbers.

Old Testament

GENESIS
Ch. 1–3 [83]
1:1–2:3 [18, 83]
1:26–27 [83]
2:4–25 [83]; *2:6* [83];
   2:7 [46]; *2:17* [37];
   2:21 [85]; *2:25* [37]

LEVITICUS
19:18 [25]

DEUTERONOMY
6:4–5 [25]
10:16 [53]
30:6 [53]; *30:11-14* [3]
32:10 [25]

JOSHUA
24:15 [47]

1 KINGS
3:28 [Preface]

JOB
3:25 [21]
Ch. 14 [15]; *14:1* [15]

PSALMS
82:6 [13]
118:22–23 [65–66]

PROVERBS
3:13–17 [63]
11:24 [88]
17:22 [82]

ECCLESIASTES
7:28–29 [23]

ISAIAH
2:2 [32]
5:1–7 [65–66]
29:13 [6]; *29:15* [6]
34:4 [111]
54:10 [111]
58:6–8 [27]
64:4 [17]

JEREMIAH
2:13 [74]; 2:13 [13]
9:23-24 [63]
17:13 [13]
29:13–14 [2]
31:33 [74]

EZEKIEL
12:1–2 [33]

AMOS
5:21–24 [13]

JOEL
3:13 [21]

MALACHI
3:2 [82]

Apocrypha

TOBIT
4:6,15 [6]

New Testament

MATTHEW
3:11 [10]
4:2 [14]
5:3 [54]; *5:6* [68–69];
   5:10–12 [68–69]; *5:10*
   [58]; *5:14* [32; 77];
   5:15–16 [33];
   5:29–30 [22]; 5:42
   [95]
6:1–18 [5]; *6:2–4* [62];
   6:4,6,18 [5]; 6:5–15
   [14]; *6:19–21* [76];

Cross-References
to the Odes of Solomon

This appendix lists all the quotations from the Odes that are included in this book.

ODES	THOMAS	ODES	THOMAS
3:5–7	2	17:13–16	Preface
3:8–9	Preface	18:11–13	3
6:6	Preface	19:1–2	101
7:7	15	20:1–4	110
8:10	62	22:12	13
8:14	22	23:4–6	47
11:2	53	34:4–5	22
11:4	18	36:1,5	101
11:5–8	13	38:1,3	18
11:10–12	37	38:10–13	28
11:12	86	38:17–18	43
12:1–3	108	42:6–9	90
16:18–20	50		
